"Emma Lauer hit a home run with her concept for *DBT Skills for Highly Sensitive People*. As an eating disorder specialist and trauma specialist for the past twenty years, I have seen all too many clients get 'over diagnosed' due to symptoms of trauma and a highly sensitive temperament. Emma's book offers a comprehensive 'how to' for these sensitive individuals to learn to emotionally regulate, practice self-care, and to reframe their sensitive nature as a strength versus a weakness or something that needs to be toned down to make others comfortable. Every therapist needs this on their bookshelf!"

— **Dawn Delgado, LMFT, CEDS-S**, eye movement desensitization and reprocessing (EMDR)-certified therapist, founder of EMDR Collective, certified eating disorder specialist with IAEDP, and EMDR-certified trauma specialist with EMDRIA

"*DBT Skills for Highly Sensitive People* by Emma Lauer is a game-changing book that is tailored toward those who identify as highly sensitive, and explains how you can apply dialectical behavior therapy (DBT) concepts toward that temperament! This book will help so many people and is a much-needed topic in the therapy space!"

— **Jennifer Rollin, MSW, LCSW-C**, founder of The Eating Disorder Center, and coauthor of *The Inside Scoop on Eating Disorder Recovery*

T0007060

"This book provides the highly sensitive person (HSP) the tools they need to access their inner GPS, and use their emotions and thoughts to help them navigate through life. Emma Lauer shows how emotional sensitivity, with its accompanying empathy and compassion, can become a gift they have been given—and a gift they bring to the world."

—**Anita Johnston, PhD,** author of *Eating in the Light of the Moon*, executive clinical director of Ai Pono Eating Disorder Programs, and founder of Light of the Moon Cafe

"*DBT Skills for Highly Sensitive People* is more than a self-help book; it feels like a hug. In a society where emotional sensitivity is considered a weakness, Emma offers a refreshing reframe. She invites us to see our sensitivity as a superpower, while offering practical tools for better regulating our emotions. If you have ever felt at odds with your emotions, don't skip this one. It will transform your life."

—**Jaime Castillo, LCSW,** therapist, founder of @findyourshinetherapy, EMDRIA-approved consultant, and author of *What Happened to Make You Anxious?*

"*DBT Skills For Highly Sensitive People* is an excellent resource for anyone who has ever felt like they're just too sensitive, too emotional, and too much. Lauer includes many easy-to-use tools that you can begin implementing today. If you're looking for a book that will help you lean into your sensitive nature and use it for good, this is it."

—**Whitney Goodman,** licensed marriage and family therapist, and author of *Toxic Positivity*

DBT Skills for
Highly
Sensitive
People

Make Emotional Sensitivity
Your Superpower Using
Dialectical Behavior Therapy

EMMA LAUER, LCSW

New Harbinger Publications, Inc.

Publisher's Note

This publication is designed to provide accurate and authoritative information in regard to the subject matter covered. It is sold with the understanding that the publisher is not engaged in rendering psychological, financial, legal, or other professional services. If expert assistance or counseling is needed, the services of a competent professional should be sought.

NEW HARBINGER PUBLICATIONS is a registered trademark of New Harbinger Publications, Inc.

New Harbinger Publications is an employee-owned company.

New Harbinger Publications, Inc.
5674 Shattuck Avenue
Oakland, CA 94609
www.newharbinger.com

Cover design by Amy Daniel; Acquired by Georgia Kolias; Edited by Marisa Solís

---

Library of Congress Cataloging-in-Publication Data

Names: Lauer, Emma, author.
Title: DBT skills for highly sensitive people : make emotional sensitivity your superpower using dialectical behavior therapy / Emma Lauer.
Description: Oakland, CA : New Harbinger Publications, [2023] | Includes bibliographical references.
Identifiers: LCCN 2023002851 | ISBN 9781648481055 (trade paperback)
Subjects: LCSH: Emotions. | Dialectical behavior therapy. | Resilience (Personality trait)
Classification: LCC BF531 .L365 2023 | DDC 152.4--dc23/eng/20230302
LC record available at https://lccn.loc.gov/2023002851

Printed in the United States of America

25   24   23

10   9   8   7   6   5   4   3   2   1   First Printing

For my clients—especially the sensitive ones

Contents

Introduction

I've seen it in my work as a therapist, and I've seen it in my personal life: those who feel so deeply that they get tangled up in their emotions, unsure of how to deal with them when they get intense, and somehow simultaneously feeling like they're both "too much" but also not quite enough. This leaves people feeling defective, when the reality is quite the opposite. These are often people that I want to grab by the shoulders and say, "But you're wonderful! I wouldn't change a thing about you." These are clients, friends, and family members who are a joy to have around because of their passion, creativity, insight, and empathy. They're highly sensitive people.

The term "Highly Sensitive Person" (or HSP for short) was coined by Elaine Aron, a psychologist who, in 1995, published a best-selling book by the same title. Aron estimates that about 20 percent of the general population fall under her definition of *highly sensitive*, which includes several specific criteria. She describes the Highly Sensitive Person as someone who is acutely aware of their environment and can carefully take in many details, including subtle cues that others may not notice, can become overstimulated as a result, and also experiences deep emotional empathy and highly emotional reactivity, meaning that HSPs feel their emotions quickly and intensely (Aron 1995).

Some parts of this may resonate for you, and some may not. Regardless of what your version of "emotionally sensitive" looks like, my hope is that this book can guide you to not only reframe how you view various aspects of your emotional sensitivity, but also learn how to use it to your advantage and wield it as the superpower that it is. I want you to own your uniqueness and see all the ways in which your sensitivity makes you wonderful as you are. Being highly sensitive is a huge gift for you and everyone around you. This doesn't mean I don't also want you to feel better equipped to navigate the inevitable challenges that come with being highly sensitive. Ultimately, I want you to feel like you have the skills needed to be as effective as you want to be in your relationships with yourself and others, at work, and in reaching for your goals. I want you to feel like you can make the most of the gifts our emotions can give us.

I want you to feel good about being someone who feels things intensely and acutely. In so many ways, it'll make your life more vibrant. I also want you to learn how to make this trait work for you, partly by identifying the ways that it might be giving you a hard time currently. What happens if you don't make friends with your emotions or learn how to work with them? Do you ever notice things coming out sideways? Do you notice coping skills popping up that are ultimately perhaps working you further away from your goals rather than toward? What are your goals, anyway? What kind of life do you envision for yourself as you walk hand in hand with this unique gift?

Dialectical behavior therapy (DBT) is the therapy that forms the basis for this book, and there are many skills from DBT that pair beautifully with the struggles typical of highly sensitive people. DBT, in turn, is derived from cognitive behavioral therapy (CBT), which is one of the most commonly used modalities in therapy and has been for decades, as it's one of the most heavily researched modalities. If you've been in therapy before, it's possible that some of these concepts—like the idea of understanding that your thoughts, emotions, and behaviors are all interconnected—will sound familiar. What makes DBT different is that it was designed specifically for those who have high emotional reactivity and tend to struggle with regulating emotions. DBT skills and HSP are a beautiful match. By pairing DBT skills with your unique needs as an emotionally sensitive person, you'll better understand your sensitivity, where it originated, and how being labeled as a sensitive person may have impacted you growing up. From there, we'll dive into more practical skills that you can use to expand your tolerance for intense emotions, put words to your emotions, and use your body to help yourself regulate. We'll also explore self-validation, relationships with others, how your physical health is connected to your emotional health, and understanding your goals and values to help yourself regulate your emotions long-term.

It's important to note that while DBT can help people struggling with many different types of issues, it's not equipped to do all the heavy lifting for some mental health diagnoses. Obsessive-compulsive disorder (OCD) and post-traumatic stress disorder (PTSD), for example, need specific treatment under the guidance of a trained professional.

As you read through this book, I recommend keeping a journal handy and using it for the self-reflection questions and exercises throughout. Take your time to work through these exercises. Sometimes the answers may come to you quickly; other times, in pieces, as you read, learn, and reflect more. Above all, just be curious. Start with some simple curiosity about what could be different, what could work more in your favor. Be open to the questions that can help you reframe how you've thought about emotional sensitivity in the past, and the skills that may help things be a little different, for the better. You've likely picked up this book because you want to feel like your sensitivity can be an asset, rather than something that feels like a defect, like it's holding you back. At minimum, I want to help you reframe that.

With the proper encouragement and tools, you can learn how to make your emotional sensitivity work for you and not against you. The skills you learn in this book will help you make friends with your emotions, understand them, regulate them so that you feel more in control, read your body and learn to self-soothe, and deal with challenging interactions with others. There's even more that I want for you, too. I want you to feel appreciated as someone who is sensitive, and I want you to be able to see your sensitivity for the gift that it is. Let's begin.

Chapter 1

Using DBT Skills to Make Emotional Sensitivity Your Superpower

Life as a highly sensitive person might be more painful sometimes, and it can also be more colorful, brilliant, and joyful. It might make you more empathetic, and more in tune with others. Your emotions are connected to your intuition, and sensitivity allows you to dig deeper into ideas and feelings that others may not be able to access as easily. Emotional sensitivity also brings a lot of passion to your life. With big feelings comes big passion. However, you may have encountered some negative feedback, or you may have had difficulty managing your emotions. If this is the case, it may be hard to recognize your emotional sensitivity as a gift. But if you happen to be born as someone who feels deeply, you can count yourself lucky in many ways. All of this is especially true when you've learned to make your emotional sensitivity work for you rather than against you. The good news is that I can teach you skills to do just this.

These skills come from DBT, and that's where we'll begin. What is DBT, and how will it help you as an emotionally sensitive person?

What Is DBT?

DBT stands for dialectical behavior therapy, and it was designed in the late 1980s by a psychologist named Marsha Linehan. Linehan developed DBT specifically to help people regulate their emotions, learn mindfulness, improve their relationships, and tolerate distress. Ultimately, she wanted others, especially those who are emotionally sensitive, to understand and learn to work with their emotions, rather than feeling like their emotions were the ones in the driver's seat.

If you've ever felt like your emotions are too big to handle or are outside of your control, it is likely that parts of this description of DBT resonate. There are all types of ways that emotions can come out sideways because they feel too big or too unmanageable to process in a healthy way, or because your options for coping are limited. And DBT has helped all kinds of people regulate their emotions and deal with all kinds of mental health struggles. A big piece of the treatment puzzle, regardless of what any particular instance of intense emotions looks like, is learning to manage emotions.

DBT teaches that emotions are messengers: they deliver us information. And the more deeply in tune you are with your emotions, the more you'll pick up on their messages. This applies even when your emotions are intense, as they are for so many who are highly sensitive people. Maybe the intensity of your emotions makes it hard to be skillful in a difficult conversation, or to help your mind and body feel calmer, or to soothe yourself when difficult emotions arise. DBT can help you learn to do these things—to make use of the messages your emotions are sending you without getting overwhelmed by their strength or unpredictability. There's even more good news: DBT skills are tangible, practical tools that speak for themselves.

In the chapters to come, you'll learn DBT skills that can help you grapple with aspects of life that you might find most challenging as an HSP. This could mean learning to manage the intense emotions that come up in relationships due to your empathy and sensitivity, to soothe the most painful or intense emotions, to be more effective in your relationships, or to feel more focused and calm in life in general. Perhaps you mostly just want regular, more stable emotions that you feel like you have a handle on. If you find that your emotions feel all over the place, or occur at random or without you being able to understand why, DBT can not only help you regulate them, but also, more importantly, help you understand your emotions so that you can befriend them rather than feeling betrayed by them.

DBT also teaches that people who are emotionally sensitive can be intuitive, creative, and make for great leaders. Again, if you're emotionally sensitive, you have a gift that others don't. You're more attuned to the messages that your emotions offer. Feeling deeply offers a richness to life that others might not get to experience in the same way, and your empathy is the foundation for meaningful, lasting connections with others. So, remember to celebrate your gifts as you move through the sometimes uncomfortable process of learning new skills.

At the core of DBT is the idea of the dialectic. "Dialectical" is a fancy philosophy word that means to explore the truth in all sides of something, by capturing the way that two things that may seem to oppose each other on the surface create a new, more well-rounded and balanced truth when they come together. For example, there are many dialectics when it comes to our emotions. I can feel excited and nervous at the same time. I can feel relief and grief at the same time. In relationships, I may feel gratitude and resentment toward someone. As a sensitive person who is in tune with your emotions, you may notice these dialectics more acutely. You really *feel* the relief, grief, excitement, nervousness, and so on that a given situation may cause—all simultaneously.

There are also many dialectics in our life experiences; for instance, I may have had a wonderful overseas travel adventure with many moments of joy and also many moments of loneliness and fear over the course of it. And finally, there may be dialectics in the things we like or value. For instance, I value safety and security, *and* I value novelty and adventure. Understanding the dialectic can be extremely helpful for you as a highly sensitive person, who might otherwise be stuck between feeling like you're "too much" for the situations you're in—like you're "wrong" in some core way for feeling things as acutely as you feel them. As an HSP, thinking dialectically will open up space and opportunity to practice acceptance of multiple truths at the same time. One way to practice thinking dialectically is to replace the word "but" with "and," an exercise taken from DBT (Linehan 2014). For example, "I feel so much and so many complicated things about this situation, it's hard to figure out just what to do—*and* my feelings, however strong they are, don't have to determine what I ultimately do." Instead of the second half of a statement negating the first half, the two halves can exist together, at the same time. When you start to think in terms of dialectics, you will find them everywhere.

Ultimately, when it comes to feeling intense emotions and having trouble managing emotions, thinking more dialectically will give you more flexibility. The situations that might feel triggering to you—a disagreement with someone close to you, noticing an intense emotion that feels disproportionate or confusing—may not seem so hopeless, and you can learn to look at things from a different angle. Painful emotions may seem a little more nuanced and less all-encompassing. You may be able to feel your experiences more fully, both the difficult ones and the beautiful ones. Thinking dialectically—and using the other DBT skills you'll learn, like mindfulness and self-soothing—gives you more options and opens possibilities for dealing with difficult situations and emotions. If you want to feel some relief from the pain that can sometimes come with being a highly sensitive person—and to learn how to use your sensitivity as the gift that it is—DBT can help.

The DBT Skills

You can think of DBT as a menu of skills, divided into four modules, or major categories: mindfulness, emotion regulation, distress tolerance, and interpersonal effectiveness (Linehan 2014). DBT skills make up the foundation of DBT, and they're what we'll focus on in this book as we go through the journey of learning to regulate emotions and harness the gift of emotional sensitivity. All four of the modules are represented throughout the book, and each of the four aims to teach a set of skills that address specific problems. But essentially, all DBT skills are about replacing maladaptive coping strategies with more helpful ones. If your current way of coping isn't working for you, or is holding you back somehow, DBT says that there's a whole menu of more effective skills that we can teach you. Not all of the skills are going to be the right fit all the time, but you will always have a large menu of options to choose from. This is where my favorite part comes in: using more helpful coping mechanisms will move you toward *building your life worth living.*

"A life worth living" means a life that is not as painful as life might be right now, and a life that moves you toward your true values and goals. If you are in what DBT calls *wise mind* (Linehan 2014), you are balancing (1) the task of acknowledging and validating your emotions—which is the task of understanding what you feel and accepting it, rather than fighting it, judging it, or trying to suppress it—and (2) the use of logic and reasoning to see, for instance, if what you're feeling is entirely accurate, or if there are other options for responding to the situations you're in than the ones that come most naturally to you. By doing this, you can be skillful, which moves you toward your goals and helps you live your true values, whereas sometimes, when we're not so skillful, the things we feel and think can lead us further away from our desired outcomes. That is what these skills can do for you.

Let's take a closer look at the four modules and the specific ways they can help.

Mindfulness

As a highly sensitive person, there's a lot that stimulates you each day. Sometimes it probably seems as though you take in everything around you, which is a lot to process, and it might feel overwhelming and hard to focus. Mindfulness, which is the ability to observe your internal experiences as they arise, without judgment, helps you to feel like you're in control of your mind, rather than your mind being in control of you. It also helps you practice having a steady focus, so that you can get the most out of one thing at a time—whether that's tending to your emotions, noticing your thoughts, being aware of what's happening around you, or being fully engaged in a conversation or an activity you love.

Emotion Regulation

You may end up using these skills the most. Emotion regulation is all about understanding your emotions, learning how to work with them, and recognizing any patterns with your thoughts, emotions, and behaviors so you can work with those too. Perhaps if you were to track your mood now, you might see a graph that over time has some dramatic spikes or dips here and there. Emotion regulation skills help to smooth that line out, leaving you feeling more in control of your emotions. Not only that, but you can better understand that your emotions are your friends, even if it doesn't seem that way now, with vital messages about what's important and what to pay attention to. With these skills, you can turn your emotional sensitivity into a superpower, rather than feeling like it's an unwieldy liability that turns on you or can be used against you.

Distress Tolerance

I call these skills the break-the-glass, use-in-case-of-emergency skills. Highly sensitive people feel distress more acutely than others. This isn't inherently a bad thing—again, feeling pain more deeply probably means that you feel wonder, excitement, and joy more deeply, too. And intense emotional sensitivity is just a trait some people are born with, the same way some are born tall. But perhaps the distress feels too intense to manage, and the skills that you've been taught or that have been modeled for you are limited. This might lead to some destructive behaviors, behaviors that move you away from your goals and values, rather than toward them. Or maybe you just find yourself in intense pain, and you don't always know what to do with it, which leaves you feeling as though you're suffering. Distress tolerance skills reduce suffering, and open space for you to respond in ways that truly serve you.

Interpersonal Effectiveness

Our interactions with others can trigger some pretty intense emotions, which is why there's a whole chapter in this book dedicated to handling these interactions in the most skillful way we can. Your true values and goals probably have something to do with having meaningful relationships with others. At the least, you want to feel as though you're living your values and reaching your goals while interacting with others. Being in tune with your emotions and using your intuition while remaining skillful will help you reach those goals and live those values.

This brings us to our first journaling exercise.

> **Self-reflection:** Consider the set of skills outlined above and the goals that you have for yourself. What are you struggling with, and what do you want to improve upon? Do you want to be more focused and in the present? Do you want to be more mindful of your emotions, noticing them without judgment? Or do you want to focus on having more skillful interactions with others while also feeling your emotions?

The DBT Assumptions

At the beginning of DBT Skills Group, we always teach the seven "DBT Assumptions" (Linehan 2014). These are the assumptions under which DBT operates as both a therapy and as a philosophy. Here are the seven DBT assumptions:

1. **People are doing the best they can.** As mentioned earlier, you're doing the best you can with the skills and experiences you have currently.

2. **People want to improve.** After all, there is a reason you picked up this book, right?

3. **People need to do better, try harder, and be more motivated to change.** This is one of the first dialectics in DBT. Both #1 and #3 are true. You are doing the best you can, and you can do more, try more. That's what these skills are: an opportunity to see if you can do more to make your emotional sensitivity a source of strength, something that works for you and that you can harness for your benefit.

4. **You may not have caused all your own problems, and you have to solve them anyway.** Situations that trigger your emotional sensitivity aren't always going to be fair. We can't control other people's actions and ways of thinking. There may also be past traumas or situations that influence your ability to regulate your emotions, and those situations are not your fault. Despite all this, can you be willing to try these skills the best you can to help make emotional sensitivity work for you?

5. **New behavior must be learned in all relevant contexts.** Just like with any other skill you've learned, being able to use these skills requires practice. And not only will you want to practice, but you'll be asked to practice in a wide variety of situations so that you can use the skills in those situations. Otherwise, your repertoire will be limited. For example, if you only ever use interpersonal effectiveness skills at work, you might find you still fall into the same patterns you want

to change when you're at home—until you start to use your interpersonal effectiveness skills in that context.

6. **All behaviors (actions, thoughts, emotions) are caused by something.** Learning to see your emotions as your friends involves learning to understand them. If you can discern the cause—the trigger, or the root of your emotions—you can feel more connected to your emotions, rather than overwhelmed by them, and you can better understand the message they are trying to send you. And your actions and thoughts are linked to your emotions too. Being aware of how all these things are connected and how they interact with each other will also help you to harness your emotional sensitivity. There's a whole skill for understanding those interactions in chapter 4.

7. **Figuring out and changing the causes of behavior work better than judging and blaming.** First, it's important to have some compassion for yourself. It's not easy being a highly sensitive person—being overwhelmed by others' emotions, or the world around you, or by the strength and intensity of what you feel and how you tend to react. And as a highly sensitive person, you might be especially aware of the consequences your emotional sensitivity can have for yourself and others. We have a whole chapter dedicated to self-validation, or the ability to recognize and honor what you're feeling just as you're feeling it, because it is vital to learn those skills as well. Not only will you feel better when you do this, but you'll find that you're more effective and skillful, too. Leaving out the judging and blaming leaves more room to understand, and thus change, any behaviors that are moving you further from your goals.

Self-reflection: How do these assumptions sit with you? As you consider this journey of learning to see your emotional sensitivity as a strength, are there some assumptions that stand out as particularly helpful? Or maybe some of which you're skeptical?

As DBT explains, we can't prove that the seven assumptions are true, but we can choose to abide by them anyway. This is practical information for you because keeping these assumptions in mind as you move through learning and applying the skills will make things easier for you. For example, when a skill feels too challenging or you feel unsure or doubtful of yourself, you can remember: "I'm doing the best I can with what I've got." It also helps to understand that in DBT, there's a fundamental belief in your ability to have more agency in your life and to be more skillful and effective.

Understanding Emotions as Messengers

DBT also teaches that your emotions are friendly visitors. They come to you with important messages. Sometimes, these visitors have a painful message that doesn't feel so friendly; sometimes they overstay their welcome for quite a while. Other times, we are thankful for whatever they're bringing. But they are never permanent. This is another gift for highly sensitive people: you have the opportunity to be in tune with many important messages, as long as you can stay aware of these fundamental facts about their nature.

Intense emotions are a cue that something meaningful is happening. DBT teaches that feeling an intense emotion can lead you to look at several important pieces of information. One would be what DBT calls *vulnerability factors* (Linehan 2014). This could be a fight with a friend, not getting enough sleep—anything that makes you more vulnerable to intense emotions. Intense emotions may also guide you to look at the event that prompted the emotion, even if at first you're not sure what specifically about that event triggered the emotion in question. The urges and behaviors that come with the emotion, as well as the automatic thoughts connected to that emotion, are also important factors. That's a lot of valuable information. There's a method for sorting through all of this, which we'll get into in more detail in chapter 4, on observing and naming what we feel.

Emotions also prompt you to take action, and they can help you communicate with others. You've maybe heard of the "4 Fs": fight, flight, freeze, and fawn. These are the four automatic responses to threats we perceive in our environments. And they reveal that emotions can be incredibly useful when we're faced with threats that require immediate action. After all, if you're experiencing intense fear and you're in danger, you don't have the time to sort through vulnerability factors or go through a whole chart exercise. Your body needs you to run, fight, do something. And those intense emotions are what gear you into action. That automatic response can also be a helpful cue for others. DBT teaches, for example, that if someone hears you shout "Run!" and hears the intense fear in your voice, they don't have to stop and think either. Your emotion has effectively communicated an important message quickly, and they'll be prompted to act, too.

The problem comes when your threat-detection system is more sensitive than it sometimes needs to be, as is the case for a lot of highly sensitive people. Or when your emotions are so strong that you end up missing the messages your emotions send you. Let's say you're giving a presentation at work and as you're talking, you notice a look on your colleague's face. There could be several automatic thoughts and emotions that pop up in response: *She's bored*; *She thinks I'm stupid*; feelings of shame, fear, or anger. And there are a few different ways things can go. If you take the thoughts and emotions as fact and act on them impulsively, you'll probably end up doing yourself a disservice. If you decide to get curious, see your emotions as information rather than fact, and use these emotions as a cue for more thoughtful action, like checking in with your colleague and asking for feedback, your emotional sensitivity then becomes your superpower.

You're more likely to pick up on these important messages if you can take the judgment out of feeling certain emotions. Some emotions get a bad rap. For example, people sometimes feel shame if they experience intense jealousy, envy, or embarrassment. Emotions are not inherently good or bad—they simply are. As we say in DBT, your emotions may not always "fit the facts"—they may not entirely fit the situation you're in— but they are always valid, based on your unique situation, your history, and everything that brought you to the point of experiencing that emotion. There's always a reason that emotions pop up in the first place, and no matter what the emotion is, it can always prompt you to look closer and find valuable information. Remember assumption #7: avoid judging. And instead, try to look at your emotions with curiosity and ask, *What are you trying to tell me?* You'll be more effective this way.

All emotions are generally an indicator that something is important to you. Not only do emotions give you worthwhile information, but they can also prompt you to go out and seek something that is valuable to you. For instance, if you do something and feel joy, you now have information about what brings more pleasure into your life. Grief not only tells you something was or is important to you, but it also helps you practice remembrance, which is vital if you're going to eventually free up some of your energy and feel less grief. Sadness helps you to seek comfort. Pain can lead to healing, and anger can be a way to find strength and feel motivation for change. These emotions are all gifts in their own way, and your emotional sensitivity gives you greater access to them.

To get to a place where you can be more in tune with these messages and benefit from these gifts, you must learn and practice mindfulness. Mindfulness means noticing what arises internally, in the present, and without judgment. This can feel like a foreign concept to people at first, and we'll talk more about mindfulness of emotions, thoughts, and urges in chapter 4, as well as skills for practicing it. But for now, keep in mind that accessing these emotions and all they have to offer requires a willingness to simply notice your emotions without judgment.

It's also helpful to remember that while your emotions have important messages to bring you, feelings are not facts. Just because you feel fear, for example, does not mean you are necessarily in danger. However, that fear is still valid, and it still has important information to bring you regarding what's happening with you internally and in your environment. The same goes for other uncomfortable emotions that we tend to shy away from, such as anger, sadness, or jealousy.

Finally, another important piece of the puzzle when it comes to understanding and regulating your emotions is being able to distinguish emotions from thoughts, and from feelings. People will say things like, "I feel like I can't do it," which is not an emotion, but rather, a thought that you have. The emotion that goes with the thought *I feel like I can't do it* might be sadness, fear, or hopelessness, and the *feeling*, or bodily sensation, might be a tightness in your chest, or a knot in your stomach. In this situation, the emotions and feelings are all valid and important to take seriously, but it doesn't necessarily mean that things are hopeless, and it doesn't necessarily mean that you "can't do it," whatever "it" happens to be. DBT skills teach you how to understand and sort through all of this.

Celebrating Your Strengths as a Highly Sensitive Person

In future chapters, we're going to delve more into why emotions are important, how to use DBT skills to listen to what our emotions are trying to tell us, and how to soothe ourselves so that we can use our emotions to our benefit. But again, our focus in this book isn't just on what you need to "fix." Now that you have a general understanding of and appreciation for how important your emotions are and all that they do for you, take some time to consider all the strengths you have as someone who is emotionally sensitive.

Creativity

In what ways has emotional sensitivity made you more creative? If you're a writer or visual artist, does your ability to feel deeply help you to create work that people can connect to? Are you perhaps more effective at conveying whatever it is you want to convey with your art? Or does your ability to feel deeply allow you to think creatively and access novel ideas?

Leadership

Some would argue that empathy is a hallmark for strong leadership. Being in tune with your emotions allows you to understand other people's emotions and experiences better, too. With these skills in hand, you can help guide others, whether it's at home, work, school, or with your peers.

Intuition

Have your emotions ever taken you someplace that you might not have had access to if it weren't for your sensitivity? What have you learned about different situations, about others, or about yourself because of being able to feel deeply and be in touch with your emotions? Perhaps you've handled a situation differently or avoided a painful situation because you could read the emotional cues.

Passion

Think of someone you know who's passionate about something. How can you tell that their feelings are genuine? What do they bring to the table with their knowledge and joy for what they love? And how does it feel to learn from and be around someone who is passionate? You likely bring the same to other people when talking about the things you love and care about. Your passion also gives you a deeper understanding of the things you care about. Has passion ever driven you to learn more about something and gain knowledge you wouldn't have otherwise?

Self-reflection: What words and ideas first come to mind when you think of emotional sensitivity as a strength? Which of these strengths we've talked about particularly apply to you? How has emotional sensitivity served you in the past? For you personally, what are the best things about being emotionally sensitive?

Building a Life Worth Living

We'll get into goals and values in more detail in chapter 8, but for now, know that learning these skills isn't always easy, so it's helpful to have some concrete outcomes in mind—things you haven't achieved quite yet that you feel will mark the fact that you're living a life worth living. The phrase "a life worth living" is a DBT concept that sometimes doesn't sit well with people. After all, your life is certainly worth living as it is now, as you are currently reading this. This is another dialectic: your life is worth living now, and taking the time to consider your dreams and what's important to you will help you feel stronger and more skillful, and it will mean less emotional suffering. Your "life worth living" goals and values are what's going to keep you motivated to learn and use these skills as you venture into harnessing your emotional sensitivity. How will your strengths as an emotionally sensitive person, those positive traits you want to keep and grow, help you to reach your goals? Will your passion drive you to learn and do more? Or will your ability to deeply connect with others bring years of meaningful relationships?

Ultimately, knowing your true values and wise-minded goals, and living in sync with them, will provide you with a sort of insurance, something to fall back on and buoy you up when those big emotions feel particularly painful, or even intolerable.

Another dialectic to keep in mind is that you are doing the best you can with the tools you have; and you can do more, do better, be more motivated to change and be more skillful. All of this is true at the same time. This book is an invitation to learn and try new skills that can move you from feeling as though your sensitivity is a hindrance to feeling like you can use it to your advantage.

Self-reflection: When you hear the words "building a life worth living," what comes to mind? Do you picture someone with healthy, close, vibrant relationships? Do you picture less emotional suffering? How does learning and using these skills to harness your emotional sensitivity move you toward a more wonderful life? Consider how DBT skills can help you build your "life worth living."

Moving Forward

The concept of emotional sensitivity as a strength may seem totally foreign to you. It's possible that not only did it never occur to you to see this part of you as a strength, but growing up and throughout your life you've consistently received messages telling you the exact opposite: that emotional sensitivity is a weakness, that it's something you need to fix in order to "be better," or stronger, or more capable. Maybe the belief that emotional sensitivity is a weakness is something that's been permeating throughout your family and culture for generations. These sorts of messages can be pretty deeply ingrained sometimes. That's why, in the next chapter, we'll explore any internalized beliefs you may have about emotions, emotional sensitivity, or your identity as an emotionally sensitive person—and the experiences that have shaped you as a highly sensitive person.

Chapter 2

Getting to Know Your Highly Sensitive Self

Do you remember the first time someone said "sensitive" like it was an insult? Was it your parent? Your friend? Or were you in a fight with a partner? Maybe you don't recall someone ever specifically saying, "You're too sensitive," but rather, you remember this general feeling of being a burden, or just too much.

I want to help you reframe whatever messages you've internalized about your sensitivity: what it means about you, your relationships, how you fit into the world. Maybe it feels like a mixed bag. Some days you love the unique way you feel your emotions; other days, the whole experience feels like a struggle. Somewhere along the way, you likely discovered that you feel things more intensely and are more affected by the world around you than others. And you received the message that your emotions are something to be dealt with rather than embraced, that the less space they take up means less mess for everyone—which has only compounded the supposed problem of feeling big feelings. In all of this, the important fact that big feelings are a gift—that they add passion, creativity, intuition, and other strengths to your life—got lost way back. One of the first steps in internalizing a new message about your unique gift is to go back to the beginning and understand how you got to this place of struggling to make friends with your emotions, starting with how you've learned to identify yourself.

How Would You Describe Your Sensitivity?

Perhaps you've always had this inkling that you're someone who's more emotionally sensitive than others, but it's never really been something you've thought much about. Or maybe you discovered the label "highly sensitive person," and it was something you latched on to immediately, something you embraced and dove headfirst into learning about. Perhaps there isn't any label that feels exactly right; it's just an intuitive sense about yourself that's always been there. Whatever your understanding of your own sensitivity, it's worth exploring how you see yourself, and the messages you're currently carrying about being an emotionally sensitive person, because everyone is different. For example, I'm someone who is sensitive and would also describe myself as logical and direct—two words that we don't typically associate with being "emotional." There is certainly room for all of this to exist at the same time, and the better you're able to understand your unique self, the easier it'll be to make room for new messages about what it means to be emotionally sensitive and the gift that it is.

> **Self-reflection:** Would you describe yourself as an emotionally sensitive person? What characteristics, experiences, or behaviors lead you to believe that you are more emotionally sensitive than others? Are there any other words that come to mind as you reflect on this part of yourself? As you notice these traits about yourself, what sorts of emotions come up? Do you notice feelings of shame, pride, embarrassment, a feeling of warmth, or something else entirely?
>
> *Also consider:* If you identify as sensitive, how did you know this? Did someone tell you? If so, who was it? What was your relationship like with this person? How did they tell you? What was the context, and what was the tone?

Unfortunately, for many people, the message they get from others is often "you are too sensitive," or "too much," and it doesn't come in the form of statements like "You're such a thoughtful friend, you really notice everything, and I so appreciate how empathetic you are." But if we can start to reframe the negative messages we've picked up in this way, it'll be easier to spot all the strengths of emotionally sensitive people. To begin this work, we'll start by trying to understand precisely where our emotional sensitivity actually comes from.

The Biosocial Theory

So, how does one get to a place where emotions feel too big to handle, sensitivity feels like a burden, and trouble regulating our emotions starts to cause problems in day-to-day life? Marsha Linehan developed a theory that explains it all, and it's called the *biosocial theory* (Linehan 1993).

The Bio Part

This first half of the biosocial theory is relatively straightforward. The simple fact is that there is a hereditability factor to emotional sensitivity. Some of us just pop out of the womb more emotionally sensitive than others. It's the way your brain is wired from the beginning, and it's in your genetics, the same as having blue eyes or curly hair. If you're more sensitive to the world around you and you feel your feelings more deeply than most, it's highly likely that you have close relatives who do, too. (Of course, how those relatives model what they do with that sensitivity is another story, and we'll get to that in a minute.) And if you've ever told yourself that you just need to try "being less sensitive," it's important to give yourself some compassion as you recognize that your emotional sensitivity isn't something you could change a whole lot even if you tried— it's in your DNA.

The biosocial theory explains that there's a biological predisposition to several factors that relate to emotional sensitivity, including quick, high reactivity (how fast and how intensely you feel your emotions in response to stimuli), slow return to baseline (how long it takes you to return to feeling calm and regulated after experiencing the intense emotion), and trouble regulating emotions (the difference between feeling like your emotions are driving the bus, versus you being the one at the wheel). All those components are somewhat predetermined at birth by various genes. Researchers have also found that one gene variant affects how vividly people perceive the world around them and how strongly they react to perceived emotional stimuli (Todd et al. 2015). This relates to empathy—your ability to pick up, be attuned to, and understand what others are experiencing is also part of your innate characteristics.

The Social Part

This is where it gets quite a bit more complicated, and where it's worth doing some serious exploration and self-reflection. Everyone's family and childhood is different and every person has their own unique set of experiences that have led to where they are now. But here's the key takeaway: the environment you grew up in and the way the people around you handled emotions has a direct impact on what your relationship with your emotions is like now. The way we approach other people's emotions and our own has so much to do with the experiences we have in our formative years. As you were growing up, the people around you taught you how to respond to emotions. We'll explore your personal experiences with this in a moment, but for now, consider: How might it be different when a person's sensitivity is taken seriously and nurtured, versus when a sensitive person is made to feel that this innate trait is a liability, an inconvenience, or worth belittling? As you can imagine, the latter doesn't spell good news. But again, every person's situation is different. Understanding your unique experiences and the environment you grew up in will help you better understand what you're struggling with and why, as well as where your unique strengths lie.

Ultimately, the biosocial theory posits that when you combine an emotionally sensitive person with an *invalidating environment*—an environment in which their sensitivity isn't recognized and normalized, in which they're instead made to feel as though their experiences and emotions are not important, not real, or not actually how they experience them—you end up with problems regulating emotions.

An environment can be invalidating in lots of ways, and we'll explore some of them. One thing that's important to note up front is that an invalidating environment isn't always the result of maliciousness. It doesn't mean necessarily that someone was intentionally invalidating. Invalidation can simply happen because of an issue with the ways we do or don't fit in the environments we're in. If an emotionally sensitive person is born into a family whose members have generally low emotional sensitivity, this can feel invalidating to the emotionally sensitive person even if everyone involved is just doing what comes naturally to them. DBT describes this condition on the part of an emotionally sensitive person as being a "tulip in a rose garden" (Linehan 2014). There's nothing inherently wrong or bad about being either a tulip or a rose. They're just different. But if you grow up feeling alone and alienated by your difference, this can lead you to feel like there's something wrong with you. Perhaps you grew up noticing that people around you didn't seem to get as mad as you or as sad as you, and when they did have intense emotions, they seemed to have an easier time managing them. As kids, we naturally want to feel that we belong. But each "tulip in a rose garden" experience you have can prevent you from feeling that. If you believe your emotional sensitivity makes you different in a bad way, or means there is something wrong with you, this can lead to a future of fighting against your emotions rather than feeling open to working with them.

For people who struggle to manage and make friends with their emotions, the direct or indirect message received from parents and other adults is often: "I don't know what to do with all these intense feelings you're having." This message can be communicated in a whole host of different ways.

How people responded to your big emotions. When you were growing up, if you cried, felt hurt, or felt angry, how did other people usually respond? How were your emotional needs met or sometimes not met? The biosocial theory posits that not only do other people's responses influence how you feel about your sensitivity and your emotions, but they also influence what behaviors are reinforced. Let's say, for example, that when you were sad or angry growing up, this generally got disregarded until things got to the point where the adults felt your emotions were impossible to ignore. Maybe they took a "cry it out" attitude, believing that your emotions would go away on their own if they didn't validate them or pay them much mind. Unfortunately, there is a prevailing false belief that emotions will get bigger or more unmanageable if they are validated and acknowledged. In fact, the opposite is true: validation soothes emotions.

And if people in your life waited until they couldn't wait anymore to tend to your emotions, what did that teach you about getting your needs met? It might have taught you that for other people to take your emotions seriously, you must take them to a level ten first. Or maybe it taught that for you to take your emotions seriously, you must wait until they get really intense and cannot be ignored any longer. Being emotionally sensitive leads people to treat you a certain way, and this is how certain behaviors and messages got reinforced, which can become a vicious cycle.

This is a key insight: how other people respond to us determines what is reinforced. If you were to cry and have big feelings as a kid, and you were met with soothing attention that encouraged you to express yourself, a positive reward would inherently come with that. And you would pick up a pattern in which you feel your feelings and then have the experience of being able to express yourself easily and to be soothed. Let's say your big feelings were ignored by others or met with frustration. What are the options then? To stuff the emotion down, only for it to come out sideways later? We don't always have the inherent ability to soothe, especially when our emotions are intense, and the ability to soothe isn't always modeled for us either. Thankfully, there are DBT skills to help give us some guidance.

There are other ways that adults in your life may have responded from a well-intentioned, but unhelpful place. Comments like "everything's okay, there's no need to cry" are invalidating. It could very well be in that moment that everything is indeed okay, and that from an adult's vantage point there is, indeed, no need to cry—but comments like this lead kids to not trust their own emotions. The situation being "okay" from that adult's vantage point doesn't change the fact that for a kid in that moment, their emotions are very real. If this is what's modeled for you, it only makes sense that it would be very hard to learn how to tune in to your emotions, understand them, and be validating toward yourself—all key ingredients for making friends with your emotions and using your emotional sensitivity to your benefit.

Defensive mechanisms and modeled coping skills. Defense mechanisms and various coping skills are modeled by the people around us as we are growing up—and there are a million and one different ways for emotions to come out sideways if we don't know how to manage them or feel uncomfortable addressing them. This means there are tons of less-than-functional coping skills and defense mechanisms we might absorb from our particular upbringings. There are about a dozen different defense mechanisms outlined by psychoanalytic theory, and some are easy to spot, such as denial (refusing to accept reality) or regression (acting younger than you are to cope). Others are a little sneakier, and if they aren't pointed out to us, we can grow up believing that they are healthy and adaptive ways of managing emotions.

One example of the latter, subtler type of coping is rationalization. In an invalidating environment, rationalization might look like this: "This problem is solvable, so what's the point of getting upset?" Or

"There's a logical reason why things happened the way they did, so this big emotional response you're having is out of proportion." Perhaps that sentiment sounds familiar? Even if you don't remember someone in your childhood responding this way, do you ever notice yourself responding to your own emotions in this way? How often do you try to rationalize away your or someone else's feelings before you've had a chance to really feel them?

And what other kinds of coping skills were modeled for you and what tools were you given as you were growing up? Anger is a common one for many of us. Anger is properly a secondary emotion, meaning that when someone experiences anger, underneath that is usually a primary emotion such as hurt, fear, or sadness. But often, the primary emotion that drives the anger is harder to discern or to really confront—both for the person feeling the anger and the people who might be witnessing it. Perhaps you saw a parent automatically act on their anger, because that came much more easily to them than explaining to you why they were hurt or afraid. Or how often did you have an experience such as this: someone had hurt feelings, but the hurt felt too big or unmanageable for them, so it was easier to just be mean instead?

What happened in your family? One of the benefits to understanding your history and how your emotions were treated growing up is to hopefully give yourself some compassion. By recognizing the patterns you've learned from the way you grew up and the history that's influenced those patterns, you can better understand how you've gotten to where you are now and what led you to have trouble regulating your emotions. The same thing is true for your parents and family members and their parents before them. What's more, unless you make an explicit point to learn new coping skills and understand your emotions better, you can only work with what you've been given and what was modeled for you. Again, high emotional sensitivity has a genetic component; if your parents didn't model healthy emotion regulation for you growing up and they didn't know how to deal with your emotions, it may be because the same thing happened to them when they were growing up—they experienced intense emotions that were invalidated, inadvertently or not, by *their* caregivers. If you've noticed defense mechanisms and other coping skills popping up in response to intense emotions, there is a reason for it—it likely felt like the only way to survive for people who didn't have much else modeled for them or offered to them, especially if they've experienced trauma. Sometimes we need defense mechanisms, and the only coping skills we've got, just to get us through a difficult time—especially if our window of tolerance for painful emotions is shrinking (more to come on that soon). If that is the case, these sorts of patterns don't change or break automatically or randomly: someone must make a conscious effort to change.

> **Self-reflection:** What messages did you receive growing up about "negative" emotions? What messages were you given about your unique traits as an emotionally sensitive person? How did people usually respond to your intense emotions? What kind of coping mechanisms were modeled for you growing up?

Messages and Values from Your Culture

On a more macro level, the culture you grew up in plays a direct role in the messaging you've internalized about yourself as a highly sensitive person. I live in the United States, a Western culture where there's a very gendered aspect to emotional sensitivity. In short, your feeling, intuitive side is considered more feminine, while your logical side that takes action instead of feeling is considered more masculine. And in turn, we're often rewarded for our "masculine" traits or actions and punished for our "feminine" ones. A woman with intense emotions, for instance, runs the risk of being called "hysterical." Of course, these are rather binary terms to be working with, and there are just as many sensitive men out there as women. Men are just as likely to be born with the "sensitive genes" discussed previously. And if you're a boy or you were assigned male at birth, and you're growing up in a culture that so often insists that people who present as male conform to appropriately "male" codes of behavior, it's likely that this was another example of an invalidating environment: an environment that made you feel as though your wonderful, natural self and its sensitivities were somehow inherently flawed. Family members, teachers, coaches, and even the books you read or movies you watched may have all been sending the message that being a boy and being emotionally sensitive was somehow off or wrong. Ultimately, in a culture steeped in sexism, behaviors or attributes regarded as "too feminine," even for women, can be deemed unpalatable—and for many of us, emotional sensitivity is one of these attributes. Even if you were rarely invalidated as a kid and these weren't messages you received directly, it's likely that your gift of emotional sensitivity wasn't nurtured or paid attention to as much as some of your other characteristics—ones that our culture sees as more "normal" for someone of the gender you were raised in.

We're also not a feeling culture in the sense of feeling with our bodies. Other cultures value connection to the felt experience of the body much more than we do. For example, many people in Western cultures are only just coming to an understanding of the emotional and mental benefits that an activity we otherwise think of as physical, like yoga, can have, despite the fact that being able to tune in to your body is a vital part of understanding and making friends with your emotions. If you cannot tune in to what you're feeling and experiencing in your body, you won't be able to identify and name the emotions you're experiencing, which will in turn make it very challenging to soothe those emotions. We'll cover skills for this in later chapters.

Sensitive Is Not a Dirty Word

Think back on the first self-reflection of this chapter. Accompanying these traits that you identified and the emotions that come up as you turned inward are the messages that you've picked up along the way about yourself. Those traits that make you an emotionally sensitive person are connected to messages you've internalized about you as a person, as someone's child, as a sibling, as a friend, as a student, as a partner. You've internalized messages about how you fit into this world and how the world will take you. Here are some examples:

I'm difficult to love.

My emotions always get in the way; I can't be effective.

I'm different; I'm weird.

My parents didn't like me.

There are direct challenges to each of these. There are people out there who believe that emotional sensitivity makes it easier to love someone, not harder. And you most certainly can be effective—that's the whole point of this book, to teach skills that will not only help you be as effective as you can but harness your sensitivity and use it to your advantage. And while your feelings of being different from others and even weird are very valid, you'll remember from the introduction that Elaine Aron identified about 20 percent of the population as falling under the category of highly sensitive people. That's millions and millions of people who have a whole lot in common with you. For example, if you believe that your parents didn't like you, there may be a very valid reason for what you feel—but it's not that you're unlikeable, or that there's something fundamentally wrong with you. It's just that you have intense emotions, and for whatever reason, your parents simply weren't well-equipped to handle them, and you were left feeling like the tulip in the rose garden.

Also, consider this: we've explored in depth places where you might have picked up negative messages about being emotionally sensitive, but what about positive ones? For example, did a teacher ever point out how creative and passionate you are? When I was little, I had a teacher who always told me she thought I'd be on Broadway someday. I didn't take this to mean that I took up too much space—it felt loving and encouraging. As I got older, I was fortunate enough to have other teachers who let me know that they saw my intuition in my writing and the comments I would contribute in class. I've learned to notice more and more when others respect my intense curiosity and passion for my interests and the things I care about. It's sometimes harder to keep positive experiences in mind than negative ones, but you should also acknowledge those times when your emotional sensitivity was seen and recognized by others as something worth appreciating, even loving; odds are there have been some.

Finally, consider that every book, movie, or TV show that you've enjoyed was very likely made by someone who was emotionally sensitive. To tell a good story, you need to understand people, and to understand people, you need empathy: the ability to tune in to your own and other people's emotions and experiences so that you can better understand them. As we outlined in the "bio" part, this innate ability to be sensitive to what others are experiencing is part of your DNA—something that can be one of your strengths, once you have the skills to use it.

Self-reflection: What messages, negative or positive, have you internalized about yourself as an emotionally sensitive person? What do these traits mean about you and how you fit into the world and with others? What do you believe about your sensitivity as a strength? Is it sometimes a gift, or always a curse? Somewhere in between?

Next: How do you want to reframe any negative messages that are working against you? Go through each message that you've identified, one by one, and come up with a reframe that uses what you've learned thus far about the strengths that people carry if they are emotionally sensitive. Reframe it in a way that feels true to what you know about your unique characteristics. For example: perhaps one of the first negative messages that comes to mind is "I'm difficult to love." What experiences contributed to leaving you with this negative message about yourself? Are those experiences the sum total of who you really are? How might your sensitivity serve as an asset to those around you? Maybe your reframe is "People are intrigued by and enjoy my passion," or "I have the ability to love others deeply."

Moving Forward

There is a reason that learning the DBT assumptions we explored in chapter 1 is an important part of starting DBT. Remember, these assumptions are beliefs that we can't prove but choose to abide by anyway as we move through a process of growth and healing. The first DBT assumption is that we're all doing the best that we can. Each person is doing the best they can with what they've been given, the lessons and experiences they've obtained thus far. Understanding and learning about where we come from breeds compassion—both for ourselves and for others. If we can better understand how we and those around us got to a place where our intense emotions feel like a fatal flaw, it'll be easier to have compassion and then move forward and makes changes that benefit us.

Also keep in mind the fifth DBT assumption, which is that we may not have caused all our problems, but we have to solve them anyway. It is not your fault if you were chronically invalidated throughout your childhood, if you experienced trauma, or if no one modeled healthy coping skills for you. And, if you have goals for the kind of life you want to live, and you want to be more effective with your emotions to get yourself moving toward those goals, it's up to you to seek out new information and make those changes—just the way you're doing now.

Again, the rest of this book will focus on helping you learn and build skills to harness your emotional sensitivity for the gift that it is. The rest is looking forward, not back. My hope is that by taking some time and attention to attend to where you've come from and how you got here, you can have more understanding, more compassion, and be better equipped to make meaningful changes in your life. Your emotional sensitivity doesn't have to be a flaw just because people always said it was. You can rewrite the story moving forward and come to understand the ways that your emotional sensitivity is a gift for you, and for others. We'll begin by diving into the first module of DBT skills: expanding your tolerance for intense emotions when they arise.

Chapter 3

Get Comfortable with Discomfort

Expand Your Window of Tolerance

How comfortable are you with emotional discomfort? The "window of tolerance" is a concept often referred to in trauma therapy, and it's exactly what it sounds like. It's your window of what you can tolerate on a day-to-day basis (Siegel 2012). Everyone has their window of tolerance for what level of discomfort they can deal with. Within that window, you'll still feel your emotions, and you'll also be alert, relaxed, able to think clearly and problem solve. Basically, when you're within your window, you're *emotionally regulated.* As you've probably gathered from all that you've read so far, being emotionally regulated means that you feel your emotions while also feeling grounded, calm, and able to make choices that are in line with your goals and values.

Of course, the window of tolerance isn't static. Your window might change day to day too, based on circumstances such as, let's say, a fight with your mom, not having enough to eat, or a poor night's sleep. What about unprocessed trauma that you've been carrying with you, or unchecked anxiety that's been running rampant? Each of these will affect your ability to tolerate distress and shrink your window of tolerance.

As an emotionally sensitive person, the gift you carry of being especially in tune with your emotions may also come with an uncomfortably small window. As an HSP, it can feel extra intense to be connected with your emotions. It might not take much to throw you out of your window. Your emotions might sometimes be felt so quickly and so acutely that it doesn't feel like you have much space to get grounded and be in your window.

If you experience something difficult and you're feeling uncomfortable emotions, you're not necessarily outside of your window—you may still be in your window, meaning you're still within the threshold that will allow you to stay regulated, grounded, and feeling safe. If so, you'll certainly still feel the discomfort but you'll more or less be able to respond from a place of being aligned with your values and goals. If you experience the discomfort and it's more than what your nervous system can tolerate in that moment, you'll either go up out of your window into a state of hyperarousal, or down out of your window into a state of hypoarousal. Trauma, or anything that's more than what our nervous system can handle in that moment, can either make us feel flooded, or shrink the world around us.

Hyperarousal is the feeling of being flooded. Your nervous system is activated, and you get pushed up out of your window of tolerance. I often use panic attacks as an example of hyperarousal. In some cases, you might not experience a full-blown panic attack, but rather, your heart is racing, you feel shaky, irritable, you're hypervigilant, having trouble sleeping, or it feels impossible to focus. You might feel like you're often tense. These are examples of hyperarousal. Hypoarousal, on the other hand, is similar in that you are pushed out of your window, but down and out instead of up and out. You feel constricted in the world around you: numb, tuned out, checked out, disconnected. Dissociation is an example of hypoarousal. Hypo- and hyperarousal are what happens when the uncomfortable, painful experiences and emotions are too much for us to bear in that moment. And if we feel as though our emotions control us rather than us being in control, grounded, and safe, our emotions start to feel less like a superpower that can be used to our advantage, and more like something unwieldly that's gotten out of hand. If we're not in our window, we lose a sense of safety and thus a sense of control. Our ability to make choices, and our ability to use our emotions to our advantage, goes out the window if we can't feel safe.

The good news is that there's a lot you can do to work on expanding your window. First, it helps to understand: How does one end up with a window of tolerance that tends to be on the smaller side versus the wider? Why is it that some people stay regulated despite difficult situations while others are easily prone to either tuning out or feeling revved up?

As mentioned earlier, day-to-day factors can play a role, including simple things like whether you've eaten enough. You can also think of the window of tolerance in terms of our sense of basic safety: if you're starving or sleep deprived, for instance, you're not having your most basic needs met, your nervous system cannot feel safe, and so your window, your space for feeling safe, shrinks. Let's say the opposite is true: let's say you're taking good care of yourself, getting your basic needs met, you've been slowly working away at healing past traumas, learning and practicing different coping mechanisms and skills for soothing your nervous system. Guess what happens to your window of tolerance? It grows, and it generally stays pretty wide.

As discussed in the previous chapter, there's also a biological component to how sensitive we are to emotions. As someone who feels things more acutely, it might take less to throw you out of your window. The gift, of course, is being in tune with these important messages your emotions can give you. The drawback is that you may need to do more to help yourself regulate your nervous system and stay in, or get back into, your window of tolerance. Any number of situations can do this. For example, maybe you've been feeling insecure about your performance at work, and on a day that started off with little sleep and a not-so-fun conversation with your partner, your boss emails you and asks for you to set aside some time to chat. Your high sensitivity means that it doesn't take much for the alarm bells to go off, and this email almost instantly has you feeling sick to your stomach, your heart pounding, and feeling like you can't think straight.

There will be times when it's biologically helpful, natural, and normal to shoot up or down out of your window of tolerance. Remember the four ways that we're biologically wired to deal with threats: fight, flight, freeze, or fawn. (One note before we go further: In this book, we'll be focusing on the first three Fs. The fourth, fawn, which refers to people-pleasing in order to avoid conflict or danger, is less relevant to hyper- and hypoarousal as they apply to high sensitivity.) "Fight" and "flight" are both examples of hyperarousal, while "freeze" is an example of hypoarousal. Let's say you're in the woods, and a grizzly bear spots you and starts to run toward you. Your heart races, your blood is pumping, and everything in your body is telling you to run. Your natural "flight" instinct kicks in, and you shoot up into a state of hyperarousal. Does that mean you did a poor job using your coping skills or that your nervous system somehow failed you because you weren't able to stay in your window of tolerance? No. Not only was it serving you well by doing exactly what it was wired to do, but it probably saved your life. The tricky stuff is when we're thrown out of our window and there isn't a real threat. That's what a small window of tolerance looks like: any perceived threat can throw you out of it. Something small and seemingly innocuous may feel like a bear charging toward you, and while the threat isn't real, the emotions still very much are.

Getting to Know Your Window of Tolerance

How much is too much for your nervous system to handle? Are you someone who shies away from your emotions, turning away from them instead of toward them? If you feel sadness, jealousy, or anger bubbling up, do you tend to stuff it down, rather than sit with it? Or when you feel these emotions, does it come out sideways in one way or another—influencing you to act in ways you might not otherwise? Perhaps some of the messages explored in chapter 2 are contributing to how you view and feel uncomfortable emotions. If you've learned that emotions are useless, just a burden, or that only weak people experience painful emotions that are difficult to manage, then why wouldn't you have a hard time when these emotions inevitably pop up? If you have that invalidating voice I mentioned earlier, notice—whose voice is that? Do you recognize it?

Self-reflection: How do you typically deal with uncomfortable emotions? Do you gear toward distraction? Do you tend to check out or find a way to numb yourself? Do you ever lash out at others, or yourself? Or do you tend to gravitate toward shaking, or a racing heart? All of us have limits to what we can tolerate. Knowing yours and what they look like gives you information, and information is power. Also consider: Do you have any theories about when or why you might've learned to cope with painful emotions in that way?

Not only are emotions natural and a part of being human, they're not harmful, either. They may feel physically uncomfortable, but that doesn't mean that listening to them will hurt you. Learning about your own window of tolerance will help you assess your readiness for making friends with your emotions and then using them to your advantage.

Self-reflection: How comfortable are you with discomfort? If you're experiencing an uncomfortable emotion, like sadness, grief, jealousy—how often do you let yourself sit with it? How often do you let yourself feel what you're feeling, rather than reaching toward distraction? And what are the factors specific to you that may make your window smaller or wider?

Start to Expand Your Window

How does widening your window and getting comfortable with discomfort translate to making friends with your emotions and using them to your advantage? Well, your emotions are going to crop up whether you want them to or not. It's a part of being human. And not only will you inevitably have emotions, but as an HSP, you will feel your emotions more deeply and more acutely than most. They might sometimes be intense, and that intensity might even feel out of proportion. But this doesn't necessarily mean that your window is narrower, if you can learn to get comfortable with discomfort. In fact, learning to get comfortable with discomfort, and learning to lean toward your emotions and say, "Yes, I'm paying attention," in a loving and validating way, will widen your window. It will create space for you to make friends and work with your emotions so that you can regulate. Perhaps you have a voice that sometimes pops up and starts to invalidate your emotions because of how intense they feel. But your emotions are inherently valid because they exist, they're yours, and they're natural. They're valid because it's your real, lived experience, and a reflection of what's happening in your body as a response to something. So why not learn to sit with them rather than pushing them away?

One helpful starting place in achieving this task is to reframe how you think about discomfort. Read this once, and then read it again: your emotions will not kill you. No one has ever died because they felt so much grief, so much sadness, so much anger, or so much loneliness. People have indeed died because of the ways they tried to cope with these emotions when it felt like more than what they could tolerate. If they haven't died, they've maybe ruined relationships, or developed dependencies on unhealthy substances or habits they'd rather break. But this doesn't happen because of the emotions themselves.

Emotions are also temporary. Contrary to what it may feel like sometimes, paying attention to a strong emotion won't prolong it or make it feel worse. That uncomfortable emotion is just trying to tell you what you need and what's important to you in that moment. Getting comfortable with discomfort, learning to ride the wave of what you're feeling and finding other ways to soothe yourself, is one of the first steps in making friends with your emotions and learning to see them as the gift that they are. It's also a key step in severing the line between feeling and then doing. If you can stay in your window and feel without necessarily acting on that feeling, you are well on your way to using your sensitivity as a superpower. Your emotion will become information that you can choose how you use. Creating a healthy window of tolerance gives you choices, as it creates space to feel your emotions without feeling pressured to act on them in that moment. Think of it as the difference between responding and reacting.

Sometimes we need to rely on a coping skill like distraction just to put our window of tolerance within reach. We can't be totally tuned in all the time; we'd exhaust ourselves. But there are drawbacks to automatically reaching toward those kinds of coping skills, rather than sitting and making friends with the emotion. First, emotions will recycle themselves if we don't take the time to feel them. Our emotions are messengers with important information about what's going on around us, internally, and what's important to us. If we don't sit with the feeling, experience it, get curious about it, and listen to what it has to say, it'll just find a way to stick around until the next time something prompts it to show up. If you tend to cope by going into a state of hyper- or hypoarousal, there's a short-term gain for a longer-term loss: you're prolonging the discomfort and saving the emotions for next time. Long term, this can look like suffering. The pain you might experience feeling your emotions is inevitable, but the suffering is optional. Your emotions need to be heard, noticed, recognized, validated, or they'll stick around until that happens in one form or another.

Giving yourself space to tolerate discomfort allows you to move through your emotions with curiosity and compassion. With compassion comes less suffering, and with less suffering comes a little more breathing room and feeling like you have the freedom and ability to make decisions. With less suffering comes free will. Learning to feel comfortable with discomfort also creates newfound ability and the possibility of putting newly learned skills into action and changing any behaviors that aren't serving you or aren't in line with your goals. This is easier said than done, and it takes practice using the skills that are coming in the next few chapters. But for now, think of approaching your emotional experience with the same curiosity and compassion that you would give to a dear friend, or a young child in your life—someone you care deeply about, and someone you're willing to be gentle with. Use kind words and patience.

Over the next few days, start to track your hyper- or hypoarousal, either taking notes mentally or perhaps keeping some notes in a journal. Look for any patterns in the ways you typically respond to situations you face. Do you notice yourself going up or down out of your window, and if so, how do you know? What do you feel emotionally and in your body? What tends to trigger your reactivity? Do you notice any patterns? You'll learn more about how to do this later in this chapter. For now, get curious about what's going on with your nervous system, and notice if you have periods throughout the day where you feel hypo- or hyperaroused. Perhaps you're wondering, *how do I know if I'm hypo- or hyperaroused and tracking the right thing?* Maybe you have some awareness around unhelpful coping skills that you tend to turn toward, or at least minor habits that in a perfect world you'd rather break. There are many, many different examples of ways that people try to soothe themselves and get back into their window of tolerance. So, if you notice that you are trying to soothe yourself with one unhealthy coping skill or another, you can track that as a time when your nervous system was dysregulated and you needed something to help put yourself back in your window. Perhaps there isn't a single unhealthy coping skill that you notice, but rather different methods of coping that you use to deal with uncomfortable feelings when they come up. In the end, with this or anything you're trying to change, simple awareness is the first step.

And—I say this often and I'll repeat it especially clearly here—try to have some grace and compassion with yourself. Trying to soothe yourself, especially if you're sensitive or prone to intense emotions, is one of the most natural things in the world, and we're all just doing the best we can with the coping skills we've got.

Skills for Expanding Your Window of Tolerance

If throughout this chapter, you're developing a sense that your window of tolerance tends to stay on the smaller side, there is good news. There are many tools at your disposal for growing your window. Some of them are small tools that you can practice right now, using five minutes of your time; others, like therapy, are quite a bit more time intensive. We'll start with the smaller stuff and then talk about more long-term solutions.

Starting Small

Just like with any other skill that you learn, sitting with your emotions takes practice. If you were learning to, let's say, ice skate, but you had never been in a rink or put on skates, you wouldn't expect yourself to get on the ice tomorrow and do a flip jump. Give yourself the same grace that you would learning anything new.

Sitting with your feelings. Start by tuning into your body. There's more to come on this in chapter 5, but for now, just start by noticing what you're feeling. Close your eyes (if it feels comfortable; if not, simply let your gaze fall to the floor or on a nearby object that isn't moving) and tune into your body. Are you agitated? Relaxed? Nervous? Sad? If you're able to name the emotion, next ask yourself—how do I know that's the emotion I'm experiencing? What's the sensation in your body? If the first description words that come to mind to describe your current state are "nothing," "calm," or "fine," spend another few moments noticing. How do you know that you're "fine?" What do you experience in your body that tells you you're fine?

Perhaps there isn't an emotion word that comes to mind, but rather, a sensation (for example: "a knot in my stomach," "a feeling in my throat," "heaviness in my chest"). That's just as well. Do the exact same thing: simply notice. Also take note of any urges that arise. Do you feel the temptation to get up, walk around, look at your phone, turn on the TV?

Perhaps you are experiencing an entirely different urge. Whatever it is, just observe it without necessarily acting on it.

Next, do you experience the sensations and urges as pleasant, unpleasant, or neutral? Regardless of whether it's pleasant or not, take a few moments to simply feel what you're feeling without judgment, without sinking into it, and without trying to push it away. Just notice it. Take a few slow, deep breaths (in through your nose and out through your mouth).

Congratulations: you're expanding your window of tolerance. With this simple exercise, you're teaching your body that you can sit with and tolerate the emotions and sensations that naturally come up. Gradually, you can work your way up to simply sitting with and observing all kinds of emotions and sensations of varying intensity. This will serve you well in situations where something triggers an intense emotion, and you want to respond rather than react.

If it feels helpful, do this exercise with a timer. If it feels at all overwhelming to do this exercise, tell yourself that starting off, you'll only have to sit with the feelings for 30 seconds, one, three, or five minutes— whatever feels comfortable starting out. Then, you can gradually increase the amount of time that you sit with and nonjudgmentally notice your emotions. Eventually, you'll be able to simply observe without acting on them for as long as you need to.

Getting Back into Your Window

Through your work to expand your window and tune into your feelings, you've also gained some awareness of what it feels like to be hyper- or hypoaroused, whether that's feeling keyed up, or a racing heart (hyperarousal), or perhaps numbed out (hypoarousal). With this awareness, you're starting to realize when you could use some tools in that moment to put yourself back into a place of feeling safe and regulated. Which tools you use will depend on whether you're in a state of hypo- or hyperarousal.

Dealing with Hyperarousal

I have a poodle-mix dog who's experienced some trauma, and it doesn't take much to send her into a state of hyperarousal. If we're out for a walk and a stranger so much as looks at her, let alone tries to talk to her, her "fight" instinct kicks in and she'll bark and bark until that person is well out of sight. Once the threat is gone, she'll do something peculiar that, if you have a dog or you're familiar with animals, you may have witnessed too: she'll shake it off. Animals have this instinct that humans don't have hardwired in the same way. They'll shake, releasing the trauma from their nervous system, and then move on once they're regulated again. One theory, informed by a therapeutic modality called somatic experiencing, is that humans develop post-traumatic stress because we're missing this natural, built-in ability to regulate. Luckily for us, there are ways that we can learn to regulate. All this means is that sometimes we must get a little crafty with how we downregulate and bring ourselves back to calm after we've been thrown out of our window. With practice, you can make this skill—releasing hyperarousal—a go-to tool in your toolbox.

One way to release a state of hyperarousal is to get your body moving. Think in terms of "shaking it off"— this could mean doing some intense exercise in a short period of time, like jumping jacks or boxing, or just dancing it out. For those of you who might actually enjoy running, going for a run can also help release and heal trauma from your body. There are also things like eye movement desensitization and reprocessing (otherwise known as EMDR). EMDR is a type of trauma therapy that's much too involved to go into in detail about here—but it relies on something called bilateral stimulation that also captures the way in which physical movement can aid us in our ability to regulate ourselves. In EMDR, bilateral stimulation can involve tapping, moving your eyes back and forth, or holding buzzers in your hands that buzz back and forth. This kind of stimulation—one that happens on both sides of the body—uses a natural, built-in mechanism in our brains to help your brain and body heal and process trauma. Before starting EMDR, I might ask my client to go for a jog and reflect on something that's bothering them, and then see how they feel afterward. Indeed, the act of running (your feet hitting the ground one at a time, your arms moving back and forth) is also a form of bilateral stimulation. My client might finish their run and discover new thoughts and emotions around whatever the issue is, and they might find that they generally feel a little calmer and more regulated. Again, this bilateral stimulation is sort of our human equivalent of "shaking it out." And again, running isn't the only way to get it; if running is something you've had an unhealthy relationship with in the past, or you simply don't enjoy it, rely on one of the many other options instead: biking, swimming, boxing—these can all have similar effects.

Other simple exercises like paced breathing (breathing in through your nose, counting to a specific number, holding for a few beats, and then breathing out through your mouth to a count that is longer than the inhale) have also been shown to be effective for dealing with hyper-arousal. That is because this exercise kicks into gear your parasympathetic nervous system, the part of your nervous system that is responsible for rest and feeling safe and calm.

Dealing with Hypoarousal

One of the dangers of automatically dipping into hypoarousal when emotions feel too painful is that you generally get used to being numbed out for the rest of your emotions, too. That's a lot of wonder, awe, joy, excitement, and important experiences and messages that you could potentially be missing out on. What is life without the opportunity to feel those emotions? How can you learn to consistently tune in to the messages your emotions bring you if your default is to tune them out? And how can you take advantage of all the gifts your emotions have to bring you if you're trying to dull your emotions? It's a waste, a short-term solution that leads to long-term losses.

If you have awareness around your tendency to disassociate, you may notice that there are a lot of times when you'd rather zone out, distract yourself from feelings and emotions, or would rather experience some numbness than feel things too acutely. If that's the case, arousing your senses might be what you need to help get you back into a window of feeling where you can be in touch with yourself and with the world around you, without feeling flooded by it.

One way to arouse your senses is to activate them. There's more to come on this in chapter 5, but for now, know that you can engage each of your five senses by tuning in to what it feels like as you engage. Something like taking a cold or hot shower, mindfully tasting one of your favorite foods, mindfully noticing what you see around you and what arouses your interest. In therapy, we call these grounding exercises.

You can try it right now with the 5-4-3-2-1 exercise: look around the room and notice five things you can see, four things you can touch, three things you can hear, two things you can smell, and one thing you can taste. This exercise can indeed also help you with hyperarousal too, if you're feeling that you need some tools that will help ground you, bring you back to the present moment, and help you feel safe. The key is to mindfully observe: tune in, be aware but not attached, noticing that your environment is safe.

Prevention Is the Best Medicine

Finally, taking good care of yourself consistently over time is one of the best ways to develop a healthy window of tolerance. There's more to come on this in chapter 9, but for now, know that being in your window means that your body feels a sense of its own safety—and in order for this to happen, your body needs to feel that it's having its basic needs met. Put another way, your body cannot feel safe if it's not being well taken care of, let alone if basic needs aren't being met. There might be some misconceptions around what "taken care of" means and what it looks like, which we'll cover later; also note that I don't mean to say achieving a felt sense of safety is all on you—your environment of course plays a role in how safe you do or don't feel, and this isn't about boot-strapping your way to feeling safe either. But for now, know that there are some basic things you can do to promote this sense of safety.

Making sure your body is getting adequate nourishment is one way. The simple act of chewing and swallowing helps your body downregulate and get back into your window because this act sends the message to your body: "I'm safe—there's enough food." This is biologically ingrained in us. What's more, a well-nourished and well-rested brain and body creates the space and opportunity for free will and creativity. There's a reason "rest and digest" is the opposite of "fight, flight, or freeze." When we're well rested and well nourished, there's room for us to think more clearly, make decisions that are true to our values and goals, and explore the gifts of our emotions. Your creativity is one of your gifts as a highly sensitive person, and it opens to you so much more easily if you are regulated and feeling safe in your window of tolerance. If you want to tap into these gifts, but exploring emotions and sitting with discomfort doesn't feel safe even on a good day, how can you expect it to go well on a day when some of your most basic needs aren't being met?

Also consider making a point to do things that bring you pleasure on a regular basis. The point of this is to mindfully enjoy these moments and tune in to what it feels like to be comfortable, grounded, and secure in your body. Get in touch with feeling good rather than zoning out and going into a state of hypoarousal. You can think of both taking care of your basic needs and doing things that bring you pleasure as insurance for the next time something comes up that might send you out of your window. Resourcing ahead of time will help you prepare for what will inevitably come up in the future, and we'll dive into how to do this in more detail later.

Long-Term Healing and the Role of Therapy

You might also find that the work you do with your emotions, as you continue working through this book, leads to especially strong emotions that you want to talk to someone about. And the more you explore, discuss, and process your emotions in a safe setting, the easier it's going to be to sit with those emotions as they come up in your day-to-day life. This is where therapy comes in. It can also mean finding another safe setting where you share difficult experiences and emotions, like perhaps a support group, or talking with a person you trust.

If you choose therapy, look for a therapist that's not only trained in traditional talk therapy like DBT and cognitive behavioral therapy (CBT), but also therapies that directly access your limbic system, which is the emotion center of your brain. Some examples are EMDR, somatic experiencing, and internal family systems, otherwise known as IFS. In both traditional talk therapy and these other types of therapy, you'll be getting in touch with your emotions in a controlled and safe setting, which will help you expand your window of tolerance in multiple ways. Talking about and exploring your emotions verbally creates tolerance through understanding (more to come on this in the next chapter), and helps you heal at the same time.

Moving Forward

Learning about your window of tolerance and how to potentially heal and grow that window is a lot to take in at once. There's a lot of potential history to consider, and a lot of factors at play, some of which might be outside of your control. If any of this feels overwhelming, that's natural and okay. Learning to expand your window takes time and practice. Also know that if for now you start with even one piece of what's covered in this chapter, it will bring you closer to healing. Next, we'll explore other skills you can pair with what you've learned in this chapter that will further help you harness the power of your emotions.

Chapter 4

Tune In to Share Your Gifts

Identify and Describe Your True Emotions

As an HSP, your emotional experience is rich. There's a lot going on, a lot for you to notice. Being able to put it into words and describe some of that richness won't just benefit you and help you to heal and work with your emotions, but it can be a gift for those around you, too. I mentioned earlier that each song, book, movie, and TV show you've ever enjoyed or felt moved by was likely written by someone who felt emotions acutely and then could translate that experience into something others can experience. That's a gift you have that you can give to others. And maybe others will share in it often, maybe it'll resonate with people some of the time, or maybe at other times it won't. Regardless, it'll feel therapeutic for you, and it'll serve you well as you learn to make friends with and understand your emotions and use them to your advantage to meet your goals or live according to your values. Being an emotionally sensitive person means that there is so much rich content there for the taking—the emotions, thoughts, insights, bodily experiences—it's just a matter of knowing what to do with that information and how to use it to your advantage. In this chapter, I will teach you a process for learning how to differentiate between your feelings and the thoughts which may cause them, as well as checking the facts of a situation. These skills will help you master your emotions, learn to release unhelpful thoughts, and be more in tune with yourself. When you learn these skills, you'll find that your emotions will give you valuable cues as to what's important to you in relation to what's going on internally and around you.

How to Use Your Cues

Knowing how to use this information to your advantage comes in two main parts: one is understanding "emotional granularity," a term introduced by psychologist Lisa Feldman Barrett that means your ability to accurately describe your emotional experience (2018). The other is understanding how your thoughts, emotions, feelings, and urges are interacting and affecting one another. Being able to identify both your emotions and the urges that can come with the emotions will also help you to learn and use the skills taught in this chapter.

It's helpful to first clarify some terminology, so that we're all on the same page. People sometimes use *emotions* and *feelings* interchangeably— but here, we'll consider emotions as distinct from feelings, or what you experience in your body. For example, I might experience the emotion of anxiety as a feeling of knots in my stomach, or the emotion of anger as a feeling of heat in my chest. Learning how to distinguish the emotions that you experience from the sensations you feel in your body, and which emotions are paired with which sensations at which times, is helpful because you begin to recognize your unique patterns and characteristics—and it'll help keep you from being overwhelmed by the intensity of what you might feel, especially at charged moments. Breaking up the experience into distinct parts helps it to feel more manageable.

That said, even with lots of practice, there's no guarantee that we'll always be able to clearly identify what's going on internally. Sometimes, you might just notice knots in your stomach. Or just heat in your arms, or your chest. This is still helpful. As you get to know yourself and your emotions more and more thoroughly, just detecting these sensations might be enough to cue you in and think, *It seems like I'm having some anxiety*, or, *It seems like anger is coming up for me*. From there, you can investigate and get curious about the emotion and thoughts you're having. As a highly sensitive person, you likely have plenty of these cues, which is incredibly helpful. We want to lean into these cues and use them to our advantage. It's just a matter of learning to tune in, give them the time of day, understand your experience, and recognize how they're affecting your behaviors.

Your *behaviors* and *urges* are also distinct and separate. If I'm sad, for instance, the behavior I engage in might be to cry, isolate myself, or maybe curl up in bed. Behaviors are observable actions. Urges, on the other hand, are something we notice in our body, but not something others can see—unless we act on them. This might be the urge to snap back at someone if you're angry, or the urge to isolate if you're sad. Noticing the difference between behaviors and urges is important because it will help you notice that you can feel an urge—even quite intensely—without acting on it.

Getting Granular with Your Emotions

Again, emotional granularity is your ability to differentiate between specific emotions and then describe those emotions with words (Kashdan et al. 2015). You may have noticed, whether it's through talk therapy, chatting with your best friend, or journaling, that you often feel better after talking about your emotions with someone you trust and putting words to your emotional experience. Neurobiologist Dan Siegel coined the phrase "name it to tame it" to help teach people from a young age that the first step in dealing with emotions is to name them so that you understand what you're working with—and indeed, there's some science behind this. The part of your brain responsible for experiencing emotions—your limbic system—is separate from the part of the brain that's activated when you practice emotional granularity and write or put words to experiences, your prefrontal cortex. Your prefrontal cortex also happens to be the logic and reasoning center of your brain. When you write about or put words to your emotions, whether that's in a journal, talk therapy, or chatting with a loved one, you're linking up the emotion center of your brain with the logic and reasoning center. As you fine-tune your description of your emotional experience, you're not only soothing the intensity of the emotion, but you're also gathering important information. It's a win-win. You'll feel better as you put words to your emotions, and you'll understand your emotional experience a little better as you learn to differentiate between different emotions and see your emotional experience as more than just "feeling good" and "feeling bad."

If you can notice and describe your emotions, you can understand them. By cluing into them, you're also more aware of the thoughts and behaviors that are connected to them, which gives you more freedom to change your behaviors, if that will be helpful to you. Your thoughts, emotions, and behaviors are all interconnected. We'll get into this more later, but for now, know that noticing and naming your emotions is one of the keys to understanding your emotions and using your sensitivity to your advantage. Your intense emotions are valuable clues that are there for you to take advantage of.

The Emotion Wheel

It might not come naturally to you to put descriptive words to your emotional experience. This is where the Emotion Wheel comes in handy. Take a moment now to hop on Google and type "emotion wheel" in the image search. You'll see dozens and dozens of colorful images pop up, all some variation of a wheel with many emotion words. Google will tell you that if you feel so inspired, you can even buy a pillow with an emotion wheel printed on it.

These wheels are generally all structured the same way: in the middle are a small set of basic emotion words that we're all well familiar with: sad, happy, angry, disgusted, fearful. Once you choose one of these words, you can narrow your selection, moving closer to the outside of the wheel and getting more and more specific with your word choice. Try it now with something you've experienced recently. Remember an emotionally intense experience that's still fresh in your mind. Next, compare how this experience feels when you pick a word in the innermost circle, compared with the outermost circle. How do you feel if you just stop at "sad," versus if you land on "isolated" or "burnt out"? One feels a whole lot more validating, doesn't it? You will be able to feel your window of tolerance opening as you give more accurate words to your emotional experience. This leads to the next important piece of the puzzle: noticing and understanding your thoughts, as your thoughts and emotions are so directly connected.

Your Thoughts Are Not Always True

Just like it is helpful to tune in to your body sensations and your emotions, tuning into your thoughts is very important. Your thoughts could be the driving factor behind those painful emotions and sensations. It is so easy to take our thoughts as facts. After all, they exist in our brains, and come up so automatically, they sure feel true. But once you recognize that sometimes a thought is just a thought, and that just because we have a thought organically pop up doesn't make it true—that can be incredibly freeing.

What's more, a thought is just a sentence running through your brain. You may notice that sometimes, if you ask people how they're feeling, they might respond with something like "I just feel like I can't do it," or "I feel like I'm going to fail." Those are not feelings or emotions. Those are thoughts. The emotions that go along with those thoughts might be something like anger, sadness, or fear. But while thoughts are distinct from emotions or feelings, the thoughts we have do influence our emotions and feelings, just as they're influenced by our thoughts and feelings. So the goal becomes to change your thoughts so that you can change how you feel, and lessen some of the emotional pain you might be facing.

How do you start working with this relationship between your thoughts, emotions, and feelings? Each of us have many, many thoughts running through our head all day long. Sometimes they're seemingly nonsensical, sometimes they're logical. Sometimes they're scary or confusing and we have no idea where they come from. This is normal. Try not to read into the types of thoughts you're having. They don't necessarily mean anything. Instead of judging them or automatically taking them as fact, get curious about how they might be connected to your emotions and behaviors.

As an emotionally sensitive person, consider that your intense emotions are more likely to clue you in to something important that's happening. Imagine it like this: first, you notice acute fear. Your mindfulness and awareness around this emotion is your first cue. From there, you can tune in to what you're feeling in your body, and sit with it. This causes you to become interested in your thoughts and any urges you're having. Where is this feeling coming from? What are the thoughts running through your head? What urges do you notice that are connected to these thoughts and feelings?

As you ask yourself these questions, you start to learn a great deal about whatever situation prompted this emotion of fear and any thoughts you're having. As you look at the situation in a different light, you're gathering so much more information about yourself *because* you feel your emotions acutely. This is another one of your gifts as an emotionally sensitive person.

Fact-Checking Your Thoughts

Sometimes, we need to check our thoughts against the facts. DBT is big on checking the facts and teaches that this is a vital skill for helping yourself regulate your emotions (Linehan 2014). This is how you'll learn more about your thought patterns and any automatic thoughts that tend to pop up, as well as understand how these thoughts might be affecting your emotions and behaviors. You can practice checking the facts and seeing the big picture by getting in the habit of asking yourself a series of questions (McKay 2019):

- What happened? What prompted the thought? A memory? Something I saw or heard? What's this thought really about, anyway?

- As a result, what did you think and feel? Be specific. Did you make any assumptions?

- What evidence supports how you think and feel?

- What evidence contradicts how you think and feel?

- What's a more accurate and fair way to think about the situation?

- What can do you do to cope with this situation in a healthy way?

Here's one example of the intensity of emotions perhaps not fitting the facts of the situation: let's say an event triggers a past trauma. Your brain's way of protecting you is to react in such a way that this present-day situation feels like life or death. If you can notice this, it makes sense to then ask: Is this life or death? Does my reaction fit the facts of the situation?

It is human nature to sometimes make assumptions; don't judge or blame yourself. Just notice it so that you can use that information to move forward. If your thoughts are based on assumptions, this is helpful to be aware of because you can then change your thoughts and thus change how you feel, or at least reduce the emotional intensity.

Opposite Action

Our behaviors, too, are closely connected to our emotions and our thoughts. Let's say you're experiencing a lot of fear around an exam or presentation coming up, and the thought is *I can't do it* or *I'm going to fail*. You might have the urge to procrastinate or avoid preparing. If you act on these urges and they end up being your behaviors, your behavior will reinforce the emotion of fear and the thought of failure, setting you up to actualize your fears. Acting on the urge to procrastinate encourages fear to stay.

If after some examination, you realize the thought or intensity of the emotion doesn't fit the facts and you want to change the emotion or lessen the intensity of the emotion, one good strategy is to do the opposite. In short, opposite action is acknowledging the urge, checking the facts, and doing the opposite if the urge does not fit the facts (Linehan 2014). In the above example, your fear is very real, and very valid, but that doesn't necessarily mean that it "fits the facts." Is there evidence that supports the thought *I can't do this* or *I'm going to fail,* and do you know those things to be certain? And another important question to ask yourself in a moment like this is: *Is acting on this emotion effective?* If you know that it's ultimately not effective to avoid or procrastinate in the face of fear, this is your cue to engage in the DBT skill of opposite action, and study for that test or prepare for that presentation, rather than avoiding it. Doing so will not only lessen the emotional intensity of whatever you're feeling, but you'll also be acting in a way that's more effective and in line with your goals.

DBT lays out some other examples of emotions, the action-urge that may follow, and what opposite action might look like instead (McKay, Wood, and Brantlee 2019):

Anger: Attack, criticize	*Opposite Action:* Validate, use a soft voice
Sadness: Shut down, avoid	*Opposite Action:* Be active, get involved
Shame: Shut down, punish yourself	*Opposite Action:* Make amends

An example might be the urge to shut down or withdraw because of feeling sad or hurt, and then reaching out, speaking up, and mindfully sharing what happened that prompted the feelings and what emotions it brought up, because you know this will be more effective in the long run.

> **Self-reflection:** As you notice the intense emotions that tend to surface for you, what action-urges go with those emotions? Do you often notice an urge to avoid, an urge to isolate, or an urge to lash out? Think of a recent example. Would practicing opposite action have been more effective for you in that situation? If so, why? And what might that have looked like?

The Model for Describing Emotions

DBT's model for describing emotions (Linehan 2014) takes everything we've learned thus far in this chapter and brings it together in one place to help you understand how these pieces interact with one another. This is particularly helpful if you end up in a situation where you feel like your emotions were running the show, led you down the wrong path, and you want to investigate so you can understand what happened. If you do this regularly, you can better understand and maybe even begin to anticipate your triggers, urges, and any patterns in behavior. In the end, it'll be something you can list on a single piece of paper, adding just a sentence or two after each section. It'll look like this:

Prompting Event:

Vulnerability Factors:

Thoughts and Interpretations:

Biological Changes (Internal and External):

Urges:

Actions:

Emotions and Emotional Intensity:

Aftereffects:

For now, we'll start by breaking it down section by section.

Prompting Event

A *prompting event* is something that triggers your thoughts, emotions, sensations, and behaviors. First, the emotion is triggered. Perhaps it's by something external: something that happened, that you experienced. Sometimes the chain of events happens so quickly that it's hard to catch what prompted the emotion. Being emotionally sensitive means that you're especially in tune with your environment. Notice whether this resonates: you hear a character on a TV show use some colloquialism that reminds you someone you used to know, someone you had a falling out with. Suddenly, you're feeling depressed. In this example, the prompting event is hearing the colloquialism. It's the event that occurs right before the emotion starts. Being emotionally sensitive and picking up on little details in your environment go hand in hand. The power in this is being able to recognize what might be causing certain emotions. Prompting events can be internal, too. A thought pops into your head, you feel something in your body, you experience another emotion. Each of these can be prompting events for emotions. There are a million different reasons why something might trigger an emotion for one person at one time, but that same situation might not trigger an emotion for a different person at a different time. Your emotional response might even change depending on the day. That's one of the reasons why it is so important not to judge your emotions.

Vulnerability Factors

Sometimes our interpretations of prompting events are affected by *vulnerability factors*. A vulnerability factor is any outside factor, such as not getting your needs met, that potentially made you susceptible to more intense emotions or distorted thoughts. Maybe you didn't get enough to eat that day. Maybe you're under a lot of stress with work, school, your family, anything. Maybe you had an argument with a family member that morning. If you're under the influence of drugs or alcohol you're also much more susceptible to emotional intensity. Maybe something else triggered you earlier in the day. The possibilities are endless. Make note of any vulnerability factors that existed at the time of the prompting event. Have compassion for yourself as you notice any vulnerability factors.

Your Thoughts and Interpretations

Tune in to any automatic words, phrases, or sentences that pop into your head because of the prompting event. Now isn't necessarily the time to challenge them or check the facts of the situation. For now, just notice and identify the thought for the purposes of seeing how each of these pieces fit together. Maybe there are a couple that stand out. Write them down.

Biological Changes: Internal and External

What do you notice happening in your body as a result of the automatic thoughts that pop up after the prompting event? Does your heart start to race? Knots in your stomach? External, observable body changes have the potential to communicate something to other people. What might you be communicating to those around you in this moment? Can you notice what facial expressions might be observable to others? What's your body language like?

Urges

What action urges do you notice in your body? The urge to flee, fight, freeze? Urges can result in observable behaviors, but only if you act on them. For example, you might notice the urge to lash out with words if someone does or says something that makes you angry, the urge to cry if you're sad, the urge to run or flee if you're afraid, the urge to isolate and shut down if you're overwhelmed. Tune into your body to notice any urges. Again, try to leave any judgment at the door. Just notice what automatically comes up for you. This is for your information, so you can use your self-knowledge as power, not for self-criticism.

Actions

Actions are behaviors that are observable by others. Maybe you acted on one of your urges, or maybe the behavior was something else entirely. If you were around other people, maybe you said something, and tried to put words to your emotions and your experience. What did you do in response to the urges, thoughts, feelings, and prompting event?

Emotions and Emotional Intensity

This is where you can put your emotional granularity skills into practice. What is the emotion word that describes what you're experiencing in that moment? Also tune in to how intense that emotion feels. Picture a thermometer, a scale of 0-100, or something like an expanding sphere. Maybe the emotion feels so intense that it's like a bubble that's about to burst. Maybe there's just a little bit of pressure. However you visualize it, get in touch with your subjective experience of the emotion.

Aftereffects

Something happened that prompted thoughts, emotions, and urges that you may or may not have acted on, as well as changes in your body as you experienced your emotions. Because of all this, there is some kind of aftereffect. Did you act on your action-urge? If so, what was the effect of that? Was the effect helpful, unhelpful? Maybe you didn't act on whatever action-urge naturally came up for you, and you were able to choose a different action instead. If so, what was the consequence of choosing a different action? Noticing the aftereffects is important because it shows you and teaches you new information about how each of these pieces end up having real consequences in your life.

Putting It All Together

Let's say you and your partner are sitting together, chatting, having dinner. Your partner makes an offhand comment about how slowly you've been working on a household project and wonders aloud whether you're having issues with focusing. Immediately, automatic emotions, thoughts, and urges pop up, and days later you're still noticing the effects of this. You mindfully take note of the emotions that are lingering and use them as a cue to tune in and take a closer look at what happened. Here's what it might look like all together:

Prompting Event: He said he thinks I might have issues with focusing.

Vulnerability Factors: Not getting good sleep lately. Stress at work. History of thinking I'm underappreciated and my hard work isn't acknowledged.

Thoughts and Interpretations: He doesn't understand or appreciate the work I do; he doesn't respect me. He doesn't care about hurting my feelings.

Biological Changes (Internal and External): Feeling hot. Feeling stiff. Arms crossed. Tightness in chest.

Urges: Withdraw. Shut down. Disengage.

Actions: Withdrew. I stopped talking as much and disengaged from the conversation.

Emotions and Emotional Intensity: Anger. Frustration. Sadness. Pretty intense. 6 or 7 out of 10.

Aftereffects: Resentment built up. We didn't talk as much for a bit. I continued to feel tense and uncomfortable. We got into a fight the next day.

As you can see from the example, if, at the end of the day, you had the experience of feeling like your intense emotions drove the bus and you didn't have as much control as you would've liked, things didn't turn out the way you wanted, or you feel generally confused about why something happened the way it did, this model can help you understand that and see how the different pieces of the puzzle fit together.

Over the next week or so, try using this model in your day-to-day life—either in the moment, when you feel your emotions rising in intensity after a particularly charged encounter, or at the end of the day, looking back on events from a place of relative calm. See whether you can use your skills of noticing sensations, distinguishing feelings, emotions, and thoughts, and considering the whole system of factors that influences how you feel and what you do to have more knowledge about and more control over your feelings and actions. Also note if you come to find it difficult to use words to describe and process what you're feeling and how you might want to respond. This isn't an uncommon experience for highly sensitive people; and in the next chapter, you'll learn other, more bodily and experiential skills you can use for dealing with these especially intense emotions and feelings.

One of the benefits to making friends with your emotions and seeing your emotional sensitivity as a strength is that you can stop experiencing your emotions themselves as an issue that needs to be solved, and instead you can look at the urges, behaviors, and aftereffects that may be getting in the way. The emotional intensity wasn't ever the issue. You are fully entitled to whatever emotions inherently pop up, at whatever intensity. Using this model helps you to see where there are some helpful opportunities for troubleshooting if the actions and aftereffects are potentially causing you distress.

Moving Forward

Ask yourself: How are the pieces of the puzzle you're currently working with moving you either toward or away from your goals? How is it serving you? Is it possibly in your best interest to shift one of these puzzle pieces in order to have a different outcome? Understanding the entire system that interacts with your emotions gives you insight into what is going on when there might be an issue. And the emotions you feel, as well as their particular intensity, are just for your awareness and information, clues as to what's important to you and what's going on internally and around you. Having compassion for and making friends with your emotions is still the goal.

With a newfound skill of naming and identifying your emotions, a world of opportunity might open up for you. How will you use the gift of describing your rich emotional experience to benefit yourself and those around you? How will you feel as you learn to describe and put words to your experience?

Emotions are a bodily experience, and as you learn all the various ways to soothe your body, more opportunities open up so you feel like you can use your emotions as the gift that they are. There are many ways to soothe yourself, and putting words to emotional experience is just one of those ways. What's more, for those of us who are highly sensitive, it may not always be the most accessible way to deal with our emotional experience. In the next chapter, we will learn skills for tuning into our bodies to further understand and calm our emotions, thus making it easier to use them to our advantage.

Chapter 5

Feel to Heal

Being in Tune with Your Body to Regulate Emotions

Sometimes, words aren't enough. That is, the ability to process using the logical, language part of the brain just isn't going to be accessible to us sometimes, especially when our emotions are really running high. When that is the case, one of our best options for calming our emotions and working with them rather than against them is to tune into our bodies and soothe using our senses, changing our body chemistry to guide us through. This is because while we can put words to our emotions—and doing so is often helpful, as we discovered last chapter—our emotions are ultimately a bodily experience. When someone says something that hurts my feelings, for instance, or if something scary happens, or if I remember a pleasant memory, I experience an emotion, and I feel that emotion in my body. Having emotions is a physical, bodily experience. It's especially so for highly sensitive people. Again, you might've found as you were practicing the skills you learned last chapter that what you feel is sometimes just too big to put into words, or the language just isn't accessible when you might want it to be. In these moments, you don't need to put words to what you feel; you can "feel to heal" instead—which means making contact with your emotions and just being with them, experiencing them in your body, just as they are. And there are plenty of skills that can walk you through how to do this. The more you practice feeling to heal, the better you will become at making friends with your emotions and understanding them. Your emotions will feel a little easier to work with, and perhaps won't feel as overwhelming. Using the skills we'll talk about in this chapter is an excellent way to expand your window of tolerance.

Interoception

Before we dive into learning the different skills, there's an important concept to cover: *interoception*. Interoception is the perception of sensations from inside your body. If you can tune into your body and feel when you're hungry, when you're tried, when you're full, when you need to go to the bathroom, when you're experiencing sadness, happiness, anger—those are all examples of interoception. It's your ability to feel what's happening in your body and then read that information.

As you can tell given the examples above, it can be very helpful information that tells you how you're doing and what your needs are. The thing is, our physical needs are generally a whole lot easier to read and then respond to. There's typically not as much baggage tied up in reading and then responding to our body's cues for basic physical needs. But when it comes to emotions, many have trouble going through that same process, despite it being just as important. Interoception is key for processing emotions, because if we cannot tune into what we're feeling in our bodies, we miss out on all the information our emotions have to offer. For someone who feels their emotions more intensely and more acutely, interoception is especially significant because it gives you more tools at your disposal. Especially when your emotions are acutely intense, you won't always be able to sort through DBT's model for describing emotions, for example. Feeling through your emotions gives you some relief when you need it most and you aren't necessarily in a place to cognitively evaluate your experience. If you are able to feel your emotions more fully by tuning into their physical aspects, you will be able to better understand them, another strength as a sensitive person.

To practice, let's start with some basic physical needs that are generally easier to identify. Take sleepiness. How do you know if you're tired? Your first thought is probably, *I can just tell,* or *I can just feel it.* But what can you feel? How do you know? Tune in and notice specifically, taking a minute to maybe write it down. A heaviness in your face? In your chest? What do you feel in your body?

Next, we'll try the same thing for a few different emotions. If you're wanting to check in with yourself, tune into your emotions and see how you're doing, you may have moments sometimes where it's hard to identify anything beyond "fine" or "content." If that is the case, see if you can challenge yourself to notice more. How do you know that you're "fine" or "content?" What does "fine" feel like in your body? I'm willing to wager that this is a new experience, as most of us don't take the time to notice what's happening in our body when we're feeling different emotions.

What about sadness, anger, or hurt? These might be examples of emotions that are more likely to need your attention when they pop up. Take a moment to notice what it feels like in your body when you experience these emotions, maybe taking down some notes to help you get more familiar.

Understanding Your Ability to Tune In

Even though it may seem simple on the surface, the above exercise is much easier said than done for many people. In the next chapter, we'll talk about the power of validation and being accepting of your emotions—but in order for you to be able to validate your emotions, you have to be able to really feel them. So for now, consider: What typically happens when your emotions pop up? Being highly sensitive means the emotions are there, and they might be loud, but how comfortable are you with feeling them in your body?

With many of my highly sensitive clients, I will ask: What's it like to be in your body? I ask because my gut tells me that it's a challenge. The emotions are there, and they are intense. Because they're intense, and because our emotions are a bodily experience, they are often overwhelming. It might even feel physically painful at times. Perhaps you can identify with the experience of learning to tune out your emotions either with various numbing behaviors or trying to think your way out of emotions instead of feeling your way through. Maybe your window of tolerance is small, which doesn't leave much space for sitting with your emotions. It takes a pretty wide window of tolerance to feel safe enough to feel our emotions in our body and trust that they won't swallow us whole.

It's important to normalize that factors outside our control can affect our ability to practice interoception and tune in to what we're feeling. If you've experienced trauma, for example, it is totally normal to feel unsafe in your body. Tuning in feels scary or perhaps just inaccessible. This is an example of when you'll need the help of a trained therapist to expand your window and heal. So, if paying attention to where you feel your emotions in your body is uncomfortable or difficult, be gentle with yourself.

I've also had plenty of highly sensitive clients tell me that they're resentful of their emotions. They're too intense; they never seem to "fit the facts" and therefore feel totally useless. I asked a client recently about what the alternative might be if he didn't get frustrated or hurt, and he told me that he would just prefer to not have these feelings at all, to which I responded, "So, you'd basically be a robot?" Obviously, this isn't an achievable goal—and if it was, would you really want that? Think of all you'd miss out on. While feeling your emotions acutely might be an intense experience, it also comes with the gifts of empathy, creativity, strong will, and the ability to tune in to whatever your emotions are telling you. I'm betting that it would be a net loss. You'd also be selling yourself pretty short if you went the robot route. Again, keep the dialectic we talked about earlier in mind: it's not your fault that you deal with more intense emotions than the average person, and you're doing the best you can to deal with it—*and* you can likely do more; you're likely capable of more than you feel you are when things are at their very worst. This too is one of our superpowers, both as HSPs and as human beings— an ability to weather more than we might think we can, when we're willing to take care of ourselves and stay open to what we experience and feel.

If you find that you tend to be all in your head, and that you've cut yourself off from feeling your emotions too much in your body, see if you can start small with these skills. Practice slowly and gradually. Trying to think your way through emotions rather than feeling your way through them might be something you've done for so many years that it'll be challenging to shift gears in a short amount of time. Try to remember that there are many benefits to be gained from letting yourself tune into your body and experience emotions. Lack of interoception prevents us from processing our emotions and letting them run their natural course. If you avoid feeling your emotions in your body, you're cutting them off at the stump and stopping them from moving through your body. Your emotions will feel stuck. And even if you can tune out the feeling for a little bit, your emotions won't back down until eventually they've been accepted and heard.

Self-reflection: What's it like to be in your body, to be highly sensitive and feel your emotions physically? Is it usually painful? Or tolerable some of the time? Give yourself some compassion as you reflect on what that experience is typically like for you.

Skills for Feeling Through Emotions

Now that you have some understanding around what interoception is, why it's important, as well as your personal patterns of either tuning in to or tuning out feelings, you can start to use skills that are specifically designed to help you sit with your emotions. Because the big ones feel really big, being able to feel through emotions (as opposed to thinking through them) will be more accessible to you much of the time. Use the skills you'll learn in this section—deep breathing, self-distraction, self-soothing with the senses, and building trust with your body over time—to not only help soothe yourself, but also to create a little more space for yourself to work with your feelings. Soothing your emotions will make it easier to practice accepting them, and acceptance is vital to not only making friends with your emotions, but also using them to your advantage. These skills can set you up to harness all the gifts that strong emotions have to give you.

Your Breath Is Always with You

Think back to what we learned in chapter 3 about the parasympathetic nervous system. Deep breaths, with the out-breath being longer than the in-breath, kick into gear your parasympathetic nervous system, which is responsible for rest, digest, and reminding your body that you're safe. Our minds and bodies are so closely linked that pairing this knowledge with interoception skills can change how we experience physical sensations.

If you notice sadness, anxiety, joy, or any other emotion that you can physically feel, tune in to where you feel the emotion in your body. Let's say you're feeling sad, and you identify the sensation as a tightness in your throat. Notice that feeling in your throat. Then take a breath in through your nose, and as you remain aware of the feeling, breathe out through your mouth as slowly as you can. Visualize the physical sensation releasing as you breathe out. Don't worry about whether the pain goes away or if the sensation changes. Don't try to force anything or push any sensations away. Just focus on feeling the sensation, breathing out, and visualizing the sensation releasing. And practice being gentle with yourself, maybe even softly placing a hand on your chest or stomach as you feel them rise and fall with your breath.

As you continue doing this, what do you notice about the sensation? Does it dissipate? Get a little softer? Perhaps feel a little easier to work with? And see if you can go through these steps again the next time you want to feel through something and help it be a little more manageable—learning to notice what you feel and be with it, maybe even to welcome it.

Change Your Feelings Using Physiology

DBT has a few handy tricks for changing your body chemistry to help bring down the intensity of emotions (Linehan 2014). I often refer to these as the "break-glass-in-case-of-emergency skills." When the emotions are so intense that it seems like practically nothing will help, try these. Remember, our emotions are a bodily experience, so using these skills gets right to the source.

Diving response (McKay 2019). In this exercise, you'll use the sharp sensation of contact with cold to disrupt any patterns of high activation and distress you might be experiencing. This one certainly isn't as pleasant as taking deep, cleansing breaths, but it will do the job if needed. This exercise will slow down your heart rate, so it's important to note that it's not advised to try this without talking to your doctor first, especially if you have a heart condition or you take a beta blocker.

You have a few different options. One is to fill a bowl with cold water (nothing below 50 degrees), take a breath, hold it, and dunk your face in the water. Hold it for a few seconds, then lift your face and let go of your breath. You can do this a few more times as needed. It's not always practical to go fill up a bowl full of cold water, so another option is to take two fingers, stick them on some ice in the freezer to get them nice and cold, place your fingers at the tops of your cheeks and then keep them there while you take a deep breath, hold it, and bend over for a few moments. If you start to feel faint or feel any pain while doing either of these exercises, stop immediately. After you practice this exercise, you'll feel your heart rate slow down, and you'll feel a little more regulated. That's because this exercise stimulates your dive reflex. If you were to actually dive into some freezing water, your body would need to conserve energy to survive, so all your functions that weren't totally essential would start to shut down. That includes an elevated heart rate due to intense anger, anxiety, or whatever the case may be.

High-intensity exercise (McKay 2019). Think back to the "shake it off" technique that we talked about in chapter 3. Moving our bodies can help release trauma or anything that shot us out of our window of tolerance, and, similarly, it can help emotions move through our bodies. Broadly speaking, sweating, elevating your heart rate, and getting those endorphins going can help you feel better mentally and emotionally. Specifically, when our emotions are at their peak, some brief, intense exercise can help us process them more quickly. It can bring down the intensity just enough so that other skills become more accessible. Think wall sits, jumping jacks, boxing, busting out some dance moves. Make it brief, just enough to expend some of that energy, and remember to breathe through it and listen to your body as you go. It shouldn't be painful. And, if you've previously had an unhealthy relationship with exercise, try a different technique instead.

Self-soothe with your senses (McKay 2019). Tuning into your body using each of your senses will not only help you practice interoception, but it will also help you process your emotions. Making gentle and curious contact with your emotions and feeling them through allows you to understand what might be causing them. Processing your emotions is so healing, especially if you haven't really made friends with your intense emotions in the past. Connecting with your emotions in a soothing way is a gentle reminder that your emotions deserve your compassion (more to come on this in the next chapter). Just because they're more intense, and just because it's painful at times, doesn't mean that your emotions don't deserve to be handled with gentle, compassionate care.

- **Smell.** Our sense of smell is different than our other senses because the part of our brain that processes smells interacts with the part of the brain that processes emotional memories. Taking a mindful moment to smell something pleasant or important to us will soothe us in ways that are just a little different from other senses. Is there a particular recipe or food that's meaningful to you? Do you have a favorite candle, essential oil, or lotion? Perhaps the memories associated with these smells are soothing in a very specific way that other senses can't provide.

- **Taste.** It is human nature to use food to soothe ourselves at times. For as long as we've been around, food and drink have not only been used as sustenance, but also for celebration, socializing, building community, and taking care of one another. Taste can be soothing in all kinds of ways, and there are a few different ways to approach this. Sometimes it's helpful to mindfully notice what food or drink has an association with something pleasant. A favorite snack, baked good, or recipe? Something that has a family connection or reminds you of your childhood, perhaps? Another thing to try is tuning in to your emotions and asking what they need. For example, if it's a comforting embrace, something warm might soothe in a way that a different food or drink wouldn't.

- **Sight.** Look at something pleasing, interesting, or engaging. Maybe it's pictures of your dog, or from a trip you took years ago. Google pictures of the cosmos or night sky and mindfully notice the details and what your eye is drawn to. Go outside and thoughtfully observe how the sky looks, whether there are clouds and the shapes they take, or look at the leaves on the trees and notice their form and texture. Google pictures of your favorite city. Flip through a book of art. As you practice each of these, pay attention to what you feel in your body.

- **Hearing.** The vast majority of us at one time or another have listened to music to help ourselves feel better or work through emotions. As with taste, you can tune in to your emotions and ask what might feel best. Maybe it's music that's quiet and peaceful, or maybe it's something more intense. Maybe it's music that's connected to specific memories or moments in time. Maybe what's soothing in that moment isn't music at all, but a different sound, like the dryer running, rain, forest sounds, waves crashing, white noise, city noises, or just mindfully taking a moment to close your eyes and pay attention to any sounds you can hear around you. If you're lucky enough to be someone who knows how to play an instrument, this is also an excellent way to let your emotions flow through your body while also tuning in to any soothing sounds you hear.

- **Touch.** What's the most tactilely soothing thing in your house? A favorite blanket? A beloved pet? The feeling of lotion (perhaps using smell and touch in one go)? Maybe a more effective and soothing way of using your sense of touch is to instead take a long, hot shower, massaging yourself, or changing into more comfortable, soft clothing. Whatever it is, the trick is to practice this mindfully, tuning in to the sensations and noticing the feelings it brings up for you.

Building Trust with Your Body Over Time

Many of the skills mentioned above are for immediate use—to use in a moment when you feel especially charged or vulnerable. But as I mentioned earlier, practicing interoception and building real trust with your body and with your emotions takes time. It takes time to practice noticing what you feel in your body and where you feel your emotions—and time to feel safe doing this. Thankfully, there are long-term options—skills you can use to build up trust and a sense of safety with your body.

Yoga and other types of exercise that involve using your whole body (think basketball, dance, volleyball, tennis, just to name a few) are examples that can help you practice. These involve tuning in to your body, feeling what's happening and then reading the cues. It also involves pairing your breath with your movement and using your breath to guide you through. Whether you're flowing through yoga poses or learning how to run down a court while maneuvering a ball, these types of activities can help you build a relationship of trust with your body. Some of us never had the opportunity to create this kind of connection with our bodies and didn't necessarily have access to sports. It is never too late to learn, and there are many different kinds of movement that can be tailored to fit whatever your needs are. Chair yoga, for instance, is easily accessible on YouTube, and you might be surprised at the low-cost sports leagues available for amateur athletes in your area.

Gradually practicing tuning in to your emotions and noticing where you feel them in your body will also build trust over time. For example, the next time you're feeling hurt, notice where you feel it, give yourself a gentle little reminder that the emotion is important and you're paying attention, maybe with a gentle "I see you," and then just breathe into it. Practicing something as simple as this often enough will teach you that you can tolerate being in your body and feeling your emotions.

See if you can track this over the next week. Commit to mindfully noticing and identifying your emotions at least once during the day. After you identify the emotion, notice where you feel it in your body. Perhaps it's a nervousness that you experience as a tightening in your throat? Or happiness that you'd describe as warmth in your chest? Once you're able to pinpoint the physical experience, practicing simply being with it and breathing through it.

Moving Forward

The skills discussed in the previous chapter (checking the facts, the model for describing emotions) can be extremely helpful for changing how you experience your emotions so that you can use them to your advantage. But your emotions weren't always meant to be reasoned through. And sometimes, your emotions will be intense enough that your reasoning skills and logic are just not going to be accessible, even if you want them to be. That's because your emotions are organic feelings. But the good news is that you can honor them as such by mindfully tuning in and simply giving them the respect of feeling and experiencing them in your body, using the skills you learned in this chapter.

All that said: sometimes we need a little more help getting ourselves to a place where practicing feeling into our emotions feels possible. Perhaps you struggle with acceptance. No matter how many tools you're given to feel into your emotions, you resent that you have to practice them in the first place, and deal with these feelings that can be so overwhelming. On a human level, this is totally understandable! But if you reject your emotions, see them as useless, or resent that they exist at all, it'll be much, much harder to get to a place where you can feel through them and soothe yourself. This is where the power of self-validation comes in. In the next chapter, we'll explore why your emotions deserve to be given the time of day, even if they don't make sense, and the ways in which they are inherently valid.

Chapter 6

The Power of Self-Validation

Give Yourself Compassion and Acknowledge Your Strengths

Self-validation—the practice of validating your own emotions and experiences—is a vitally important tool in your HSP toolbox. To be validating of yourself or someone else means that you simply acknowledge your or their emotion or experience, and you're accepting of the reality of that emotion or experience. It's a magic tonic that might not always go down smoothly, especially if you're new to practicing it, but in the end, it'll soothe emotions in a way that not many other skills can. That's because your emotions inherently want and need to be heard and acknowledged. They're here with important messages, after all, about what you need and how you're coping. And even if they are painful, feel inconvenient, don't "fit the facts"— they are still valid. They're valid just because they exist. They're the natural reaction to your experiences, which makes them inherently legitimate.

Having particularly intense emotions might mean that you need that extra reminder at times that you're entitled to your emotions, it's okay to feel them, and they're valid. Perhaps you've noticed that when it comes to dealing with friends, family, and acquaintances, validation feels like second nature. Telling someone that it's okay to feel their emotions, that their emotions make sense, and that they're doing a great job—this kind of compassion might come very easily when it comes to caring for others. But when it comes to caring for yourself in this way, all those skills somehow fly out the window and you're much, much harder on yourself than you would be toward anyone else. If that sounds even a little familiar, that's a sign that you could really use a refresher on what it means to be validating, how to practice validation, and more importantly, *why* we practice validation. By going over why this is such an important skill, you'll be able to see all the opportunities you have to benefit as an emotionally sensitive person.

Self-validation can soothe and thus bring down emotional intensity enough for us to get curious about and then work with our emotions. It is not only kind and compassionate, but it's practical: the more you practice, the easier it'll be to work with your emotions. As an HSP, practicing self-validation is the difference between intense emotions that become more intense and more painful, versus intense emotions that feel soothed with the knowledge that they're being taken seriously.

In this chapter, we're going to highlight the difference between validation and invalidation, bust through any myths you have about validation, and then dive deep into various skills you can use to practice self-validation. By using these skills, you can soothe your emotions, which creates space to practice all of the other skills learned in this book. Not despite, but especially because you are a highly sensitive person, you deserve the same warm, compassionate, and caring words that you might give to a loved one. When emotions are running their highest, this is especially the time to show up for yourself by offering validation and acknowledging all the work your emotions are doing for you.

Validation and Invalidation: What Do They Look Like?

I often find that people think they know what it means to be either validating of themselves or someone else, but then struggle to put the skill into practice. That's because people sometimes get hung up on the question of how they can be validating if they don't understand precisely why someone (including themselves) feels the way they do, or if they firmly believe the emotion a person is feeling should be different from what it is. Here's an example. Let's say your partner comes home from work and tells you they had a really hard day because of a problem with their coworker. They felt pushed aside at work, and they're feeling angry and frustrated. Perhaps you're listening and you immediately jump into problem-solving mode, trying to find a practical solution for your partner. Or you may be thinking to yourself, *I don't understand why you didn't just tell your coworker what you needed*, or, *That doesn't sound like that big of a deal to me*. That's fine, and those things might be true. It also doesn't have to impact whether you're able to be validating toward your partner in that moment. Even if you don't understand the emotions of anger and frustration, you can still say, "It's a horrible feeling to be pushed aside when you're trying to do your work." How do you think your partner will feel in response to one statement versus the other? The later, the validating statement, will soothe and create a safe space for exploring more. The former, the invalidating statements, will likely cause your partner's emotions to feel more painful, and will shut down the conversation. With some time, your partner is probably very much capable of coming up with a practical solution—especially if you validate their right to sit with their pain for a second and have it be heard before they move to solutions. To jump over their emotional experience and head straight to problem-solving feels invalidating because it misses the point in the moment. The same is true for your relationship with yourself and your self-talk. First and foremost, acknowledge your feelings. They are meant to be felt, they exist for a reason, and the intensity is a strong cue to tune in and listen to what they're saying. When you feel intense emotions popping up, do you jump into problem-solving mode, try to rationalize or shut them down? How aware are you of how you communicate with yourself when strong emotions arise?

If you're chronically invalidating toward others, it might become obvious to you more quickly than if you're chronically invalidating toward yourself. Other people might call you out on it, it might come out sideways in more arguments with your partner, or you might notice that your relationships don't feel very trusting or safe. But if you're invalidating toward yourself and haven't realized it, or you haven't taken the time to change your patterns: consider this your callout. At the very least, you deserve to treat yourself with just as much kindness, compassion, and empathy as you give to those around you.

One way that people often invalidate their own emotions is with the sentiment "I shouldn't be feeling this way." Perhaps, as someone who feels things quite deeply, you believe that your emotions are often out of proportion to the situation. You believe that you feel *too* sad or *too* angry when something triggers these emotions. Like we talked about in chapter 4, it may be the case that your emotions are connected to a distorted thought that doesn't necessarily "fit the facts." If you're able to recognize when this is the case, it might make your emotions particularly frustrating, because you know that they aren't proportional or fitting to what's happening around you. But that doesn't mean that your emotions are wrong or bad. Your emotions are the natural response to whatever triggered them, and because they are the natural response, they are inherently valid.

Let's say you reach out to a friend to make plans and she doesn't respond for a while. The timeframe in which she usually responds comes and goes, and you start to have automatic thoughts like *she doesn't like me enough to spend time with me.* The emotions that come along with this are probably pretty crummy feeling. You might feel sad, hurt, disappointed, maybe even embarrassed. Because you're highly sensitive, you feel these acutely and intensely. Logically, you know that there are a million and one reasons why she might not be responding. You know better than to take it personally, so your feelings are frustrating.

There are a couple of important things to consider here. One is that your emotions are an automatic reaction. You didn't sit down and consciously choose to feel hurt and embarrassed. Emotions are your birthright, as they're a natural part of being human, of being you. Your emotions just are what they are. Trying to fight them or get down on yourself because they don't make sense right away or because they feel inconvenient won't change that. The other, perhaps more important thing to recognize is that by invalidating your emotions, you may be missing out on the important message they're trying to bring. This friendship is important to you! Building close friendships and spending quality time with others is part of your values system, and it's in line with your lifelong goals of having quality relationships. So of course this feels important. *It makes sense.* We'll get into this process more later when we explore skills for self-validation. For now, use this example to recognize that just because the emotions don't fit the facts doesn't mean that they're wrong or bad.

Types of Validation

Validation can come in many forms. Often, we think of validation as the words we say in response to someone, or our self-talk, and these are the examples we've looked at thus far. But validation isn't just the words you tell yourself or someone else. There are many ways to be validating, and having a wide array of options for doing so will make it easier to practice. Let's go through some of them now.

Showing that you're listening. Give yourself and those around you the respect of showing that you're paying attention and that you're genuinely interested in their experience. If someone is upset or trying to share their feelings with you, drop any distractions, and give them your full attention. Do your best to focus. If you're having painful emotions pop up, do the same for yourself: drop any distractions, tune in, and pay attention to your emotional experience, which includes your thoughts, feelings, emotions, and any urges. Let's say you're at home spending some time with yourself and you notice your thoughts wandering toward something that happened at work. You feel a little anxious, frustrated, maybe sad. Then you notice the urge to turn on the TV, or the urge to spend an indefinite amount of time scrolling through Instagram. As mentioned previously, there can be a time and place for distraction. It can be helpful when the distress is really, really high and you need something that can bring it down to what feels like a manageable level. But in a situation like this, can you challenge yourself to tune in and turn toward, rather than away from the feelings? Can you take advantage of this time to listen and show yourself that you're listening, paying attention, and ready to validate?

Reflecting. Reflecting to yourself and others—restating what you've heard them say so they can confirm you're correct—is inherently validating because it shows that you're making an effort to understand what you're hearing. While reflecting to someone else, don't worry so much about whether you get it right. The other person can correct you and tell you more accurately about what they're experiencing. Hearing that you're making an effort, and then having the chance to share more about what they're feeling, will be soothing on its own. As for reflecting how you're feeling to yourself, know that our emotions inherently want the chance to express themselves, and we have an inherent desire to put words to our experiences. Once you do, sit back and see if your words feel right or if they don't. Think about the emotional granularity skills explored in chapter 4. Exploring the nuances of an emotion and describing the experience feels validating and is soothing.

Stating what hasn't been said out loud. This is part of reflecting. Do more than just state back what the other person has said. For example, if someone says their feelings were hurt, you may do more than simply state back, "it sounds like your feelings were hurt." Put yourself in their shoes, for even a second, and see if you can identify more about what they might be feeling and experiencing. Can you understand why their feelings were hurt given the situation? How might you feel if you were in their shoes? "It sucks to feel like someone's behaving disrespectfully toward you. I'd be angry too."

Using validating body language. Sometimes so much as a grimace, a sigh, or a sympathetic look on your face can be deeply validating. It shows that you can understand the emotion, at least to some degree, or maybe there's a part of you that empathizes. Practice body language that conveys openness, which often means actions like turning toward someone, making eye contact, and sitting with your arms uncrossed.

Applying Validation Skills to Yourself

If you know what validation for and from others looks and feels and sounds like, it can be easier to give it to yourself. Notice how you feel when someone else is paying attention, interested in your emotional experience, and tells you or shows you that what you're feeling makes sense. Now imagine being able to do the same for yourself with your own self-talk. Imagine how that may change your relationships with your emotions, and create space to work with them, rather than feeling like they're working against you. First, we'll take a closer look at some of your patterns and history when it comes to validation and invalidation, and then we'll be sure to bust through any lingering myths you might hold about self-validation, before finally moving on to practical ways that you can practice this and apply it to yourself.

Your Patterns of Validation and Invalidation

Dig deep within yourself and be honest: Do your emotions ever come out sideways because it feels like the only way to validate them? For example, maybe you go binge drinking after you failed an important exam or got into a fight with your best friend. Maybe you've previously lashed out at someone because they hurt your feelings. Sometimes it feels like a big response is the only way to get validated, especially if we haven't given ourselves the tools to do this for ourselves. The emotions end up coming out sideways, because they haven't been properly acknowledged, and the unconscious thought process becomes: *I must take this to a level ten for people to see how much pain I'm in. If people can see how much pain I'm in, then I can finally feel validated.* Behaviors that are the result of misdirected emotions likely aren't working you closer to your long-term goals—and as you can probably guess, using self-validation skills is going to be more effective for you long term. This is also another pivotal moment where compassion and empathy for yourself, and awareness of the dialectic, are required. We're all doing the best we can with the coping skills we've learned thus far. And there are ways we can do better, once we have the right tools.

Facing our emotions head-on and giving ourselves validation is going to be especially hard if there isn't a good history of others being validating toward our emotions. This goes back to what we learned in chapter 2. Just like the adults in your life modeled for you how to approach big emotions, they also modeled (or didn't model) validation. Be gentle with yourself as you approach skills that weren't modeled, haven't been practiced much, or are generally new to you.

> **Self-reflection:** Was there anyone in your life growing up who helped show you that your emotions made sense and were worth taking seriously? How did they do this? Did they reflect to you what they saw and heard? Was there anyone who paid special attention and worked to understand what you were experiencing when you had a big emotion? On the other side of things, did you experience a lot of invalidation growing up? What did that look like?

One of the best ways to learn the difference between validating and invalidating statements is to notice your previous experiences with validation and how it made you feel. By noticing patterns in your interactions with others and the ways you deal with your own emotions, you can notice what has felt soothing and comforting. This gives you some guidance for how you can give yourself this same soothing comfort. For example, maybe you have a dear friend who has given you full permission to feel your emotions in the past, telling you things like "it's okay to feel angry about this," or, "it's okay to feel sad." Use this voice to do the same for yourself, reminding yourself as needed that it is okay to feel whatever emotions naturally come up for you. This becomes significantly easier if you can also work to break down any myths that you're harboring about validation.

Debunking Myths About Validation

One of the most common myths about validation I come across is the belief that acknowledging or paying attention to the emotion is going to make it feel worse, make it more intense, or prolong the feeling. People run into this both with themselves and with other people. I sometimes hear people say things along the lines of, "If I tell this person that I understand they're upset, then they're not going to acknowledge how unreasonable they're being." It doesn't matter if you think that someone else, or yourself, is being unreasonable. That part is irrelevant to whether you can be validating in that moment. Emotions are always inherently valid, so when in doubt, you can validate the emotions. But there is likely some aspect of the person's experience that you can also validate.

Something important to remember about validation is that we only validate what is valid. Validation does not necessarily mean that we agree with every aspect of the way a person's responding to something. For example, if someone is telling you that the sky is green, validating them doesn't mean that we go along with that statement. It means that you can have a conversation about it while acknowledging that perhaps it makes sense they think that, depending on their experience. Maybe that's what they grew up learning. In that case, of course it makes sense they would believe that. Regardless, we can validate that as a true experience for them.

Think back on the example at the beginning of the chapter. If someone came to you and said that they were upset about their friend not texting them back in a timely manner, and you jumped into explanations about how that's not logical and they weren't being reasonable—that would feel deeply invalidating. It would be missing the point. It may be true that the response isn't logical. But focusing on the valid part of the experience—the hurt feelings, given how much they care about the friendship—will help soothe hurt emotions, and by doing so will open space to then maybe sort through the logical side of things.

Because your emotions so desperately want to be heard and acknowledged, it's more effective for validation to come before any problem-solving or reasoning through the issue. Validation does the opposite of prolonging the emotion. It can help drive people closer to seeing a different side of things, not further away.

Finally, validation soothes emotions, which gives you more space to feel safe, regulated, relaxed—and creates room to notice what your emotions are trying to tell you so that you can work with them. By feeling emotions more intensely, you have the gift of the opportunity to explore what your emotions are trying to tell you about what you need and how you're doing. And, at the very least, it's an opportunity to give yourself the compassion and empathy that you deserve.

Skills for Self-Validation

Practicing self-validation can be broken down into several parts. This first includes practicing acceptance by identifying your emotions and reminding yourself that it's okay to feel them. Then, see if you can acknowledge why you feel the way that you do. See if there's an opportunity to tell yourself, *it makes sense.* Lastly, acknowledge what you're doing well, and see if you can understand your responses and behaviors—and determine how you might *want* to respond, given what you most value in a particular moment or situation. We'll dive into each step further below.

Acceptance

The first step in self-validation is to start practicing acceptance of your emotions. All that we've talked about thus far in this book has primed you for this. Remembering that your emotions are your friends, even if they're painful, and that they exist to bring you important messages, will make it easier to accept your emotions even if you don't understand them or you're not happy with how it feels. It is a common, normal experience for people, both highly sensitive and not, to have emotions pop up that they would rather do without. People have thoughts like *I don't want to feel angry about this. I don't like the way it feels. I wish I wasn't so angry.* As a highly sensitive person, this experience is more acute, because you really feel the emotions as they come up—even the ones you wish you could do without.

Being able to use your emotional granularity skills from chapter 4 by naming your emotions is another important step in acceptance. Simply being able to say, "I feel angry. I'm disappointed. This was disappointing for me." Whatever it sounds like, acknowledge the reality of your experience and start there. Remembering that you are entitled to your emotions can make it easier to accept them. They're a normal part of your experience, and being highly sensitive and feeling these emotions more intensely doesn't change whether you're entitled to them. This sounds like reminding yourself that anger, sadness, jealously, or any other typically uncomfortable emotion is not inherently bad. It is okay to feel these emotions. It does not mean anything bad about you. It is a natural part of being human to feel a wide array of emotions.

Acknowledgment

The next step is to see if you can acknowledge why you might feel the way that you do. Does it make sense in some capacity? Think back to the example at the beginning of the chapter of feeling disappointed and hurt because your friend hasn't responded to your text. Sure, you may be jumping to conclusions, but it still makes sense that you feel the way you do because the friendship is important to you. Also, no one wants to feel left out or rejected, so if those are the kinds of thoughts running through your heard, then of course it makes sense that you would feel that way. The simple words *it makes sense* that you feel this way can be deeply validating.

What's Working Well

Sticking with the example at the beginning of the chapter and putting yourself in those shoes, consider, is there anything positive you can glean from that experience? Reaching out to your friend in the first place is a positive thing, given that you care about and you're trying to maintain the relationship. What you might need in a situation like that is some compassion and a little reassurance that you tried your best and didn't do anything wrong. If you have trouble gleaning something positive from the experience, remind yourself anyway that you're deserving of empathy and compassion. Remind yourself too that you can handle big, painful emotions. Not only are they something you can handle, but being sensitive and acutely aware of your emotions is a strength as it sets you up to more easily practice the skills you've learned.

Self-reflection: Think of a recent time when you were struggling with your emotions, or your emotions felt too big to manage. What are some self-validating statements that could've worked, or could work for you in the future? What helps you to feel most validated, and what feels soothing in those moments? It might be something as simple as, "This is really hard. It's okay for it to feel hard right now." Sometimes, when things are really painful, there simply aren't words. This is a reason to have some simple reminders that you can fall back on.

Moving Forward

Getting in the habit of responding to yourself in a validating way is challenging, especially if there's a long history of doing the opposite. But people who are highly sensitive need this skill and these reminders even more than those who are not particularly sensitive. It soothes those intense emotions and leaves more space for you to use the skills that will help you be the most effective you can be. Self-validation can give you some much needed relief when relief feels hard to come by.

By accepting, acknowledging, and having compassion for yourself, you can more easily tap into what your emotions are trying to tell you; you can use your emotions to better understand your experiences and what's important to you, and you can work with your emotions to use them to your advantage. Being able to channel your experiences and your values more easily is a gift. Learning more about and practicing validation will also take you a long way in aiding your relationships with others. Being sensitive means that you're naturally more in tune with others and have the ability to empathize more easily. Validation is just one of the skills that can help you in having the best relationships possible—a topic we'll explore more in the next chapter.

Chapter 7

Stay Centered with Others

Soothing Reactions So You Can Respond from Your Truth

There's no getting around it: we're social beings, and we need our relationships. When relationships are rocky, or when things feel askew with family or closest friends, it can wreak havoc on our mental health. Being a highly sensitive person can make you especially prone to interpersonal sensitivity, meaning that you are in tune with others to the point of being deeply impacted by their emotions and behaviors. This also means that feeling supported, valued, and feeling as though you have open, honest communication with the people you care about can do wonders for how you feel day-to-day. Having healthy relationships frees up space for you to be yourself, to pursue the passions and goals that are important to you, and to do it while feeling empowered, calm, and centered.

Relationships can be a big trigger for someone who is emotionally sensitive. Perhaps you've noticed that it's one of your biggest triggers: your day might be going swimmingly until someone makes a comment that your brain runs with, or someone's tone gives you a sinking feeling in your chest. On a regular basis, someone may intentionally or unintentionally do or say something that brings up some pretty intense emotions. And that's okay. Regardless of the reason or what happened, you are entitled to your emotions, and again, your emotions are always valid. Sure, they may not "fit the facts" as we say in DBT, but you're just as deserving of your emotions as anyone else. And we can't stop emotions from popping up in the first place—all we can do is self-validate, self-soothe, and control how we respond. Your emotional sensitivity also brings so much to your relationships. People in your life can likely feel your deep care and passion for those you are close to.

Now that you've learned general skills for understanding your triggers, your emotions, thoughts, urges, and how they are all connected, as well as ways to self-validate and self-soothe, you're armed to take on the most difficult interactions—at least, up until the part where you must either approach a conversation or respond to someone. This can be one of the most challenging aspects of our relationships with others: knowing how to set boundaries, avoid assumptions, ask for something or tell someone "no," and be both gentle and firm. Of course, DBT has skills for all of this.

The DBT interpersonal effectiveness skills are comprised of three main categories: skills that help you reach your objective if there's something you need or want, skills for maintaining your self-respect, and skills that help you to maintain your relationships. You can use skills from one, two, or all three of these categories at a time. Which skill or skills you use depends on what your main goals are for the interaction. There will likely be plenty of situations, for example, when your main goal is to ask for something, but the relationship is also very important to you. In this case, it's easy to use multiple skills at the same time, as you'll see once we go into them in more detail. Which skill you focus on the most will depend on your main priority. We will also cover how to stay grounded when we have painful or uncomfortable feelings toward other people. For the emotionally sensitive individual, this might be one of the most helpful skills. This final set of skills teaches how to soothe and approach the situation from a different light when our emotions toward someone are running the show and impacting our ability to be effective.

Goals for Being Effective in Your Relationships

Each person's goals are going to be different, depending on their unique needs and characteristics. Maybe you're someone who knows how to be very gentle and validating, but you have a hard time getting your needs met. Or perhaps you have a hard time not letting difficult emotions take over while you're in the midst of a heated conversation. Below are three main goals for learning and using the interpersonal effectiveness skills (McKay 2019):

1. Assertiveness in getting what you want and need from others. You deserve to have your needs met, and to be able to ask for your needs in the most effective way possible.

2. To build healthy relationships by listening and being mindful of those around you. Being emotionally sensitive means that your relationships are probably very important to you, and having strong relationships is likely part of your values system. Your strengths as a highly sensitive person set you up to have strong relationships, as your sensitivity can make you keenly aware and more tuned in to those around you. You can harness these strengths and use them to your advantage as you work to be more mindful in your relationships.

3. Negotiation. Finding a balance (again, going back to dialectics) so that you can take a wise-minded approach to your relationships takes both skill and practice. Being able to negotiate means that you're balancing both your emotions as well as reason and logic, because both are equally important. This could also mean balancing short-term needs with your long-term goals. Overall, having balance and being able to negotiate in your relationships will help them go the distance.

> **Self-reflection:** What are your main goals for your relationships? In what areas do you want to improve?

What's Getting in Your Way?

Before getting into the skills, DBT teaches that it's helpful to explore various factors that may be impacting your ability to be effective with others. If you haven't explored some of these hurdles or worked to reframe the myths you're carrying about relationships, then the skills are going to be very hard to use. First, let's start with some examples of various factors that can get in the way of being effective with others (McKay 2019):

1. **Old habits.** You've been doing things a certain way for a very long time, perhaps decades. The ways in which you deal with conflict were modeled for you growing up by various adults, and if no one ever taught you or modeled effective interpersonal skills for you, how could you know how to use them, or know to do anything differently?

2. **Emotions.** Fearing your emotions or fearing an emotion-driven reaction to someone, or not knowing what to do with painful emotions when they pop up, can all contribute to lack of interpersonal effectiveness. This is where the skills learned in earlier chapters come in handy. If you know how to soothe and validate your emotions, and see them as important messengers, they won't get in the way of your relationships. Instead, they will help. Your emotions have important information to give you about everything in your life, including and especially your relationships.

3. **Failure to identify your needs.** It's hard to get what you want if you don't know what you want. Identifying your goals and your needs will help you be effective with other people, and will help you balance not asking for too much or too little.

4. **Fear.** This goes back to chapter 4, when we learned mindfulness of thought and understanding how our thoughts interact with our emotions and behaviors. Practice recognizing the worry thoughts that are causing fear and thus getting in the way of your relationships, so that you can talk back to the worry thoughts and turn them around. If you do this, you can reduce the fear you feel in relationships, and in turn be more effective.

5. **Toxic relationships.** We can't control how other people behave and think. We may have some influence by being skillful, but at the end of the day, all we can do is stay mindful, validating, and use our skills to the best of our ability. If someone else is unwilling to do their part, or they trigger you to the point of it being very hard to use skills, it is of course going to be very difficult to be effective in that relationship. There will be times when relationships aren't serving us well, but they cannot be avoided (like perhaps that with a family member, or someone you work with). In cases like these, the best you can do is redirect yourself back to what you can control, like your skills use.

Self-reflection: In those times when your interpersonal skills are less than perfect, what gets in the way the most? Is it feeling overly responsible for other people's emotions? Your own intense emotions? Is it the worry thoughts? Or do you simply need some more skills practice?

Interpersonal Myths

Over the years, many of us have internalized myths about interpersonal relationships. You may not be consciously aware of the myths you're carrying. Sometimes, these myths are told to us directly through our culture, our family, or indirectly through modeling. Let's say you grew up with an adult who rarely asked for help, exercised stoicism at all costs, and would collapse in shame before they finally admitted to needing a helping hand. In this case, how easy do you think it would be for you to ask others for help? What do you think your views would be about others who are vulnerable or ask for help? All of this might be programmed into you without you being consciously aware. Again, intense emotions can distort our thoughts, and make distorted thoughts feel very true, which is why it's especially helpful for people who are emotionally sensitive to be aware of these myths.

DBT teaches that the best way to unlearn these myths is to come up with your own challenges against them, and then practice taking that myth to task. For example, if you grew up believing that asking for what you need makes you weak, remind yourself of your challenge against that myth: practice asking for your needs. Then watch as you build your relationships and get your needs met without people thinking you're weak.

Whether you believe each of the following myths or not, practice writing your own challenge for each of the following four common myths of relationships (McKay 2019):

1. Myth: If I need something, it means there is something wrong or bad about me.

2. Myth: I won't be able to stand it if the other person gets mad or says no.

3. Myth: It's selfish to say no or ask for things.

4. Myth: I have no control over anything.

Some of these may not resonate at all, while others may resonate quite a bit. Perhaps you had a difficult time coming up with a challenge statement for a few of these myths. If you did, that's okay—the point is to start with recognizing some of the myths that you're holding. Awareness is the first key to change.

> **Self-reflection:** Which of the above myths are ones that you have internalized, and how have they impacted your relationships? How have they impacted your ability to get what you want or need?

The Three Core Skills

In this section, we'll explore three skills key to interpersonal effectiveness in DBT: getting what you want and need (which also involves learning to say no effectively), maintaining relationships, and maintaining your self-respect.

Getting What You Want and Need

Asking for something or saying no effectively is sometimes a lot harder than it seems on the surface. Intense nerves, any of the myths outlined above, or sometimes simply not knowing where to start can all get in the way. The following exercise essentially gives you a script. It walks you through, step by step, how to approach the conversation, and it's broken up into two parts: one being some internal reminders you can use to carry out your script effectively, and the other being building the script (what you're going to say). If you've ever learned "I" statements, that's essentially what this is: more elaborate "I" statements.

When you first start out using this skill, it can be helpful to write out what you want to say. I had a client who wrote out a whole script before an important phone call with her dad. After the skill has been learned and practiced, you'll start to use it without thinking about it much. For example, staying mindful in the conversation is a big part of this exercise. With practice, this is eventually something you won't have to remind yourself to do.

There are infinite scenarios in which one might use this skill. For example, let's say someone has been teasing you or making jokes about your sensitivity, and you want them to stop. The first piece of the skill is to learn the internal reminders that will help you be more effective in your ask or saying no. The three internal reminders are: mindfulness, confidence, and flexibility.

1. **Mindfulness:** Stay mindful in the conversation. Don't get distracted by worry thoughts or anything else going on around you. Stay focused. Is this challenging for you? What usually distracts you the most or makes it the most difficult to stay mindful in interactions with others?

2. **Confidence:** Make eye contact, speak clearly, stand or sit up straight. Regardless of how you feel on the inside, doing these things will help you to feel more confident. Perhaps there is someone who, whenever you interact with them, for whatever reason, really weakens your confidence. Being aware of this will help, and staying mindful will, too.

3. **Flexibility:** In some instances (like those relating to safety), there might not be much room for negotiating or flexibility. In other situations, a compromise might be possible. The

general idea is to be open to others', ideas and comments, while also staying focused on your needs. See if there's a way for everyone to leave feeling satisfied. In this example, you can express a willingness to meet the other person where they're at by stating something along these lines: "I think you probably mean well, and I do get it if teasing is just your sense of humor or your way of relating to someone."

It may be helpful to practice these three skills in other interpersonal situations so that when it comes time to ask for something or state "no" clearly, it will be easier to stay focused and confident. For example, perhaps start implementing more mindfulness in your conversations. Practice this now and see how it gets easier with time.

The next piece is to build your script. These are the communication steps you would follow:

1. **State the situation.** The first step is to ask yourself: What is the situation? State the situation as simply as you can and using only the facts. You want to make sure everyone is on the same page and knows what's being talked about. In this example, it might sound something like: "I've noticed lately that you've been making jokes about me being too sensitive."

2. **State your feelings using I statements.** Step two is to state how the situation makes you feel using an "I" statement (i.e., "I feel..."). "I" statements keep the focus on yourself and on your experience. "You" statements (i.e., "you're always such a jerk") may set the other person up to get defensive. For example: "I feel hurt and embarrassed when you make those kinds of jokes."

3. **State your need.** Step three is to assert your need, or firmly and clearly state "no," if that is your goal. Put your ask out there clearly, or say no clearly so that the other person knows exactly what it is you want or need. For example: "I would really appreciate it if you didn't make those kinds of jokes anymore."

4. **Reinforce your request.** The last step is to reinforce your request (or your "no") so that the other person knows why this is important, and why they should grant your request. It may sound something like: "If you stopped doing this, I think I'd enjoy our time a lot more. I generally really like hanging out with you, and our relationship is important to me. Also, I see my sensitivity as a strength and something that helps me in a lot of ways, and not as a weakness."

I've seen this skill used for all kinds of situations: a teenager wanting a new phone, saying no to taking on another project at work, asking for a ride home from a party. The possibilities are endless. It's okay if this skill is hard for you. Talking about hard things and trying to have healthy relationships with others isn't easy, and everyone experiences their own unique challenges when it comes to relationships. One thing to remember is that as an HSP, you have so many gifts to bring to the table. Being an HSP friend, partner, or family member means that you are intuitive, caring, empathic, and passionate. You can use these skills to be effective while at the same time also bringing your gifts to the relationship.

It's also quite possible that you're already using a lot of these skills in your day-to-day life. As you take a closer look, maybe you find that you were just missing the "mindful" piece, given that emotional intensity can be distracting. Or maybe you were missing stating "just the facts" at the beginning. Maybe it's usually easy for you to make your ask or say "no," and you don't really have to think about it. But, if you find that doing either of these feels difficult, or you're not getting the results you want, using the above skills together can help make sure that you have all your bases covered.

> **Self-reflection:** Are there specific situations in your life in which this script could be helpful? Which part do you need the most practice with? Consider a situation currently in your life in which you want something from someone and you would like to get your needs met. Write out a sample script of what you might say, and include cue words or reminders for yourself that will help you stay mindful and confident.

Maintaining Relationships and Self-Respect

People tend to fall toward one end of a spectrum or the other. In this case, at one extreme, some people have a hard time maintaining relationships, while at the other, some are people pleasers and have trouble maintaining their self-respect while in difficult interactions with others (Linehan 2014). Of course, reality is a bit more nuanced than this, and perhaps you find that you move along the spectrum depending on the situation.

If you tend to fall toward the first end of the spectrum, you may find that it's hard to maintain relationships because being gentle and validating toward others doesn't come naturally to you. Perhaps validation wasn't modeled for you throughout your life. Or perhaps intense emotions were frowned upon and you were never taught how to process them in a healthy and effective way. If this is the case, not knowing what to do with emotions can translate to being coarse in response to other people's emotions and needs. These are the kinds of problems I see most often with emotionally sensitive people who have trouble maintaining the relationships in their lives. Perhaps there are pieces of this that resonate with you. For the purposes of learning this next skill, let's say, for example, that someone has a problem with something you recently said or did, and they approach you with their own thoughtful "I" statements and skillfulness. Here is how you can practice with a three-step approach:

1. **Get curious.** The first step is to get curious about what is going on with the other person. Rather than jumping to conclusions (which we'll talk about more later in this chapter) or defaulting to defensiveness, choose to be interested in the other person's experience. Even if you're not interested, pretend. It will do wonders for your relationships if the other person feels you are interested and care about their experience. In this example, it might sound like this: "Tell me more about how you felt when this happened," or "Tell me more about the thoughts you were having after I made that comment."

2. **Validate.** Step two is to validate. Use the skills learned in chapter 5 to do this. Remember, validation does not mean that you necessarily agree. You can still validate someone's emotions, opinions, or struggles, even if they don't "fit the facts," just like you can for yourself. Many people worry that validation will reinforce unwanted behavior, and this is a myth. It will only help to soothe and move the conversation forward, just like validation for yourself can do for you. One of your strengths as an emotionally sensitive person is your empathy, and you can totally use this to your advantage in step two. It might sound like this: "I can understand why you felt worried after this happened," or, "I know that it's awful to feel disrespected by someone close to you."

3. **Be soft in your approach.** The third and final step is to make sure that you approach the conversation with gentleness, and an easy, light manner. Be temperate in your approach. Avoid sarcasm (which can sometimes be a defense), judging, or blaming. Smile, have an easy tone of voice, use a little humor. Think soft shell over hard shell. Think strength in softness.

Think of a recent situation in which you could have used this three-step approach. Spend some time reflecting and writing out how you could have used the above skills to be more effective in your approach.

On the opposite end of the spectrum, perhaps you've noticed that there are certain people or situations in your life that leave you feeling flustered, like you couldn't stand up for yourself, get your needs met, and as a result you don't feel as good about yourself by the end of the interaction. This next set of skills is geared toward helping people maintain their self-respect in situations like these (Linehan 2014). If you're emotionally sensitive, it's possible that you've struggled with a sensitivity regarding others' emotions, feeling overly responsible for them, and maybe assuming you know what other people are feeling. This can lead to things like over-apologizing, and not wanting to commit to your needs because you worry about "rocking the boat" or upsetting other people.

Let's say that a friend said something that bothered you, and you want to make sure you come out the other side of the interaction feeling like you stood up for yourself and made your needs known. Here is how to practice:

1. **State your honest needs.** Step one is to consider your honest needs. Don't lie about or underscore your needs, pretend that you're helpless, make excuses, or exaggerate. Be honest and straightforward about your needs, and about the

situation. Just state simply what bothered you: "That comment you made felt disrespectful and hurt my feelings."

2. **Be fair.** Step two is to consider both sides of the story and both people's needs. Be fair to yourself and the other person. Your needs and feelings are just as important as theirs. In this example, it means feeling confident that you can state how this situation felt and that there's space for you and the other person to state their feelings and desires.

3. **Don't apologize.** Step three is to make sure you don't apologize for your needs and your values. If you don't have anything to apologize for, then you don't need to say "sorry." You don't need to preface asking to have your needs met with "sorry," and you don't need to apologize for having emotions or your values. It's okay if this feels uneasy—you can tolerate difficult emotions. Your values are worth sticking to even if it's uncomfortable. You don't have to change your mind or apologize about something just because the other person appears upset or has emotions come up in response to your needs and values. It might sound something like this: "I understand that this is maybe uncomfortable and that you're not happy to hear that I didn't like what you said, but this is important to me, and I care about us having a respectful relationship that feels good for both of us." Internalizing these messages will help you reach your goal and fulfill your desire of having healthy, happy relationships.

Now, it's time to practice. Think of a recent situation in which you could have used this approach. Spend some time reflecting and writing out how you could have used the above skills to be more effective in your approach.

> **Self-reflection:** Which end of the spectrum would you say you learn more toward? How does your emotional sensitivity impact your ability to practice these skills? How can your emotional sensitivity help you to practice?

Changing Your Thoughts to Change How You Feel About Someone

This next skill is arguably the one you may gravitate toward the most as a highly sensitive person. This skill is meant to be helpful when an interaction with someone else has you feeling upset or dysregulated and unhappy with them (Linehan 2014). Being sensitive to others can sometimes lead you down a path of making assumptions and letting your thoughts get carried away with you, which in turn can make uncomfortable emotions about someone feel even worse. Intense emotions can distort your thinking. Your emotions running the show may also lead you to reacting from an emotion-minded place. As you can imagine, an emotion-driven response (as opposed to a rational-minded response) is unhelpful a lot of time and will often move you further from your goals. The good news is that while being emotionally sensitive can sometimes make interactions with others more difficult, it will also make it easier for you to use the following skill. You'll see how as we move through an example of how to practice it.

This skill is broken up into two parts: the first being the cognitive piece, meaning that you're changing your thoughts toward the situation or person, and the second being the emotional piece.

The Cognitive Piece

Think about the situation from the other person's perspective and consider what assumptions you are making. What might this situation be like for them? What kinds of emotions might they be experiencing? Are their emotions valid or understandable, even if you don't agree? Using your mindfulness skills, notice what's going on with the other person. This may help you change how you think about the situation. For example, how does the other person look? Are there moments where they're trying to be kind or making an effort? Or does it seem like they're struggling?

Be mindful of your thoughts. Are you perhaps jumping to conclusions, mind-reading, or thinking of the worst-case scenario? How might any emotions you're experiencing lead to distorted thoughts about the situation or how the other person is behaving? More importantly, is there a different interpretation that might help you approach the situation from a more wise-minded place?

To practice this, think about a recent, difficult interaction with someone that you don't necessarily have warm feelings toward. What are some alternate ways of thinking about the situation?

The Emotional Piece

This is where your strengths as a highly sensitive person will really come into play. Use your sensitivity and compassion to have empathy for the other person. It will help get you into a more balanced perspective as you prepare to respond from your truth and communicate effectively. Practice kindness in your response and approach. You can stick to your values, and to getting your needs met, while also being kind, gentle, and validating.

In the interaction you described above, how could you have used your strengths as an emotionally sensitive person in order to feel better about the situation and toward that person?

If you are consciously practicing the above skill, you might find that it actually comes naturally to you as a highly sensitive person. This is an instance where your sensitivity is not only a gift for yourself, but also for the other person. Your sensitivity allows you to tap into your empathy and kindness, and other people will be able to feel that from you. As a sensitive person, you can give these gifts from a truly genuine place. Other people will also have the opportunity to see your unique insights. With practice, you are capable of mindfully noticing your emotions as valuable information, then taking that information to make new inferences and interpretations. A highly sensitive person can intuit more and see different sides of a situation.

Moving Forward

These skills are a lot to take in all at once. Figuring out which ones fit your specific needs and struggles will be a process. As discussed in the DBT assumptions in chapter 1, these skills must also be practiced in a wide variety of settings to get the hang of them. You must practice them in the context you want to use them in. If you tend to have problems with your family, but you only ever practice the skills at work, then it's probably going to continue to be hard to communicate well with your family members. Give yourself the opportunity to learn these skills in different contexts so that you can feel prepared to do your best no matter the situation. With enough practice, these skills will eventually become second nature.

Many of your strengths as a highly sensitive person are internal gifts—ones that you get to enjoy for yourself day in and day out. But as you make efforts in your relationships, and as you connect more to other people, they will also benefit from your gifts. If given the chance, others can appreciate your empathy, unique insights, and your contagious passion for your goals, values, and interests. Relationships will likely play a major role in your long-term plan for both regulating your emotions and using your emotional sensitivity as a strength. The more skillful you can be in your relationships, the better set up you'll be for a long-term happier you.

Chapter 8

Filling Your Cup

Accumulating Positive Experiences to Fill Your Emotional Bank

Two words have come up again and again throughout this book: values and goals. That's because understanding your values and goals is central to DBT and using the skills that you've learned. Your values and goals are what will guide you as you learn and practice new skills, and they're what will make the skills feel worthwhile. Your values and goals are unique to you, and as you do the work in this chapter, you'll have a guide for building up your emotional bank that's tailored just for you. It's another tool for managing your emotions, particularly when they feel too big to manage, and helping them work for you.

Your values are your standards for yourself and the principles that you use to shape what you do and what you prioritize in your life. Your goals can be short-term, long-term, related to relationships, work, your art, your travel—anything. The first step will be to think about what gives you pleasure and makes you feel good on a day-to-day basis. As you can imagine, being conscientious about doing more of this will help you feel better in the long run. The next step is to get in touch with your values and what's important to you. You'll probably see that there's a connection between your values and what you enjoy doing on a daily basis. These both tie in with your goals. Your values inform your goals. Lastly, you'll spend some time recognizing your short- and long-term goals. With both your values and knowing what makes you feel good as a guide, you can set yourself up to feel better emotionally long term and more confident as you work toward what's important to you. You'll see that your values and goals also highlight your strengths, and your sensitivity isn't your only strength.

At the heart of DBT is what I refer to as DBT's tagline: the concept of "building a life worth living." Marsha Linehan even used this as the title for her memoir. We touched on this concept in chapter 2. Your life is currently worth living, and also, what can you do to go above and beyond and make it feel like you're not just surviving but thriving? With your values and goals as your compass, you can construct your life in such a way that you're working toward the things that are uniquely important to you, and that has you saying to yourself, *Yes, this was worth all of the hard work.*

Helping your emotions feel regulated consistently over the long term is particularly important for someone who is emotionally sensitive, because regulating your emotions can be challenging. Emotions feel bigger and thus a little unruly at times and difficult to tame. Your sensitivity also sets you up to be more, well, sensitive to those vulnerability factors we talked about in chapter 4. Anything you can do to help regulate your emotions over the long term can be thought of as a sort of insurance that protects you from vulnerability factors or whatever else pops up that perhaps triggers intense emotions. And doing the work in this chapter is building on the theme of recognizing your strengths. As you accumulate different kinds of experiences, you will get more and more in touch with all you have to offer the world, both as a sensitive person increasingly in tune with the world around you, and as someone who has a wide range of other types of strengths and talents, too.

What Brings You Pleasure?

Your pleasure is important. As a culture, we're getting a little better at recognizing this, but some of us still have some work to do in this regard. You probably already know the clichés: you can't pour from an empty cup, and put your oxygen mask on first before helping others. How often do you prioritize doing something simply because it makes you feel good and brings pleasure to your life? Simply put, you will feel better and be in better shape, emotionally and physically, if you are regularly engaging in activities that bring you pleasure. You will feel energized and more resilient, and you are putting in good, hard work to take care of yourself if you regularly make time for this. When you feel better, working with your emotions, making friends with them, and using them to play to your strengths as a sensitive person are going to be so much easier. This will make it more easeful to do the work that's important to you, maintain the relationships that are important to you—basically, the things that are connected to your values and goals. It's all related.

DBT teaches that accumulating positive experiences, both short term and long term, will build emotional resilience (Linehan 2014). First, I'll walk you through how to identify the activities that can help you build this resilience, and how to work them into your schedule in a way that's realistic and sustainable. You'll come up with a plan so that you can bank up some of this emotional resilience, thus helping you to feel even more confident in your emotions working for you and serving as one of your biggest strengths.

Start by making a list of the activities that you already know bring you pleasure. Jot down lots of different kinds of activities in your journal, considering ones that require more planning and energy and those that don't, activities that you can do even if you're having an off day or feeling down. There's a big difference in terms of energy expenditure between, say, watching a movie versus taking yourself out for a picnic in the park. Also consider activities that require spending some money and ones that don't require any money. Come up with your own ideas first, and if you need more ideas to keep you going, you can take from this sample list:

- Take yourself out to get your nails done.

- Take a bike ride or a walk through your neighborhood.

- Rewatch a beloved movie or episodes of your favorite TV show.

- Take yourself to the movie theater (or the regular theater).

- Try a new baking recipe.

- Look at art online, in a museum, or in a book.

- Volunteer with animals or at a local food bank.

- Get a professional massage.

- Sit in a coffee shop or restaurant and write a short story, poem, or song.

- Practice an instrument.

- Read a book or read articles on a topic that interests you.

- Play a game with your pet or try to teach them a new trick.

- Have a bonfire.

- Drive to another neighborhood and look at the houses.

Your list will be unique to you. Only list the things that genuinely bring you pleasure, even if it's very different from what someone else's list might look like, or someone else might not understand why something on your list would bring you pleasure. You may also have to put effort into trying different activities before you figure out what you genuinely enjoy. This can be hard at first and it might require getting comfortable with a little bit of discomfort (think back to the chapter about your window of tolerance). Unfortunately, some activities (like playing an instrument, for example) won't always feel easy or come naturally to you on the first try, and they might cause some serious discomfort before they bring any pleasure. We call it "building mastery" when you practice, put in the effort, and make the commitment to try it anyway. When you work to get better at something over time, the short-term discomfort will ultimately bring long-term joy, pleasure, and satisfaction. Not only will your new hobbies and activities bring you pleasure, but the act itself of building mastery will bring confidence and pleasure. So, if you feel like you don't really have any hobbies, or you feel overwhelmed with the idea of trying or picking up something new, take heart in knowing that building mastery will pay off in many ways. Having a variety of interests also makes for a wonderful, colorful life.

One of the keys to doing this successfully is to engage in these activities mindfully. Bring balance to your life by doing these things with mindfulness. If you're hustling and pushing yourself to constantly go, and aren't prioritizing taking care of yourself, you won't experience much pleasure, and your emotional bank is going to run dry much more quickly. And, if you're mindlessly watching TV for good chunks of the day, this probably isn't bringing much pleasure to your life, either. Balance is important for the highly sensitive person. Being an HSP means you're also more sensitive to burnout, and if you're not proactive about managing it, it may sneak up on you.

Lastly, figure out how you're going to work something from your list into your regular routine. Commit to doing something from your list regularly. My recommendation is to start small. It is ideal that you make time to do something pleasurable every day, but if you're not mindfully enjoying something from your list on any day of the week, it's going to be hard to do this. So, start with one day a week. Commit to doing something from the list on Saturday, and once you've gotten in the habit of doing that, add another day. Mark it on your calendar, or set a reminder on your phone. If you want to go above and beyond, see if you can track how these activities affect your mood. At the end of the day (or the next), after taking time for yourself to do something from your list, jot down some notes about your mood, your sleep, and your energy levels.

It's important to validate that focusing on pleasurable activities can feel like a luxury, and maybe one that's not always afforded. It may be hard to think about integrating more of this into your life if you feel like you're struggling to meet your basic needs, or if you have too many responsibilities on your plate. One of my hopes for you is that even if this is the case, you're still able to start somewhere, on a small scale if needed, and take even just a few moments to use your mindfulness skills and bring more pleasure to your life using the resources you already have within you and around you.

Your Values

Your values are unique to you, and how well you understand your values and then integrate them into your life will leave you feeling more contented, emotionally stable, and satisfied by life. It's going to fill your emotional bank to the fullest, and it's the first key to building your "life worth living." The fuller your emotional bank is, the easier it will be to see your sensitivity as a strength and use it to your advantage. A full emotional bank will serve as protection from intense painful emotions, helping them feel a little more manageable when the going gets tough.

It's important to be honest with yourself as you assess what's truly important to you. That's the only way you'll get the most bang for your buck as you fill up your emotional bank. It's okay and normal for values to change over time. We grow, mature, learn new information, have new experiences and different needs. My values of adventure, creativity, honesty, and kindness have generally stayed the same, while I value, for example, financial stability a whole lot more now than I did when I was a teenager. My husband valued consistency and routine throughout his life, and after he started to travel more, the columns shifted a bit and he started to value and prioritize novelty more than he had. These are examples of how your values and priorities may have changed over time, too. For this reason, it may be worth revisiting the following exercise periodically.

The Values Exercise

The following exercise is informed by acceptance and commitment therapy (ACT), which largely focuses on knowing your values. On the next few pages, you're going to see a list of values. Grab a pencil and two different-colored highlighters (or three different-colored pens, or whatever three different writing utensils suit you). You're going to divide the list into three categories: "not important," "important," and "very important." First, use the pencil to cross out the values that you consider not important to you. If this is hard for you and you struggle to identify values that aren't important, you can skip this step. Next, use two different colors to categorize and group the values that are "important" and "very important" to you.

Then, look at your "very important" category, and use the pencil to circle the values in this category that you feel you have some control over. It may not be something that you can control outright, but if you feel you have some semblance of control over some aspect of this value being in your life, go ahead and circle it. You'll be left with a list of values that are very important to you and that you feel you have some control over. Spend a few moments looking at what you have highlighted and circled. Consider any themes you notice, words you circled that perhaps surprise you, feelings that come up as you look at these words. Also consider—are there any values missing from this list that you want to add?

Accomplishment	Fairness	Modesty
Abundance	Faith	Money
Accountability	Family	Nature
Accuracy	Flair	Nurturing
Achievement	Flexibility	Obedience
Adventure	Forgiveness	Open-mindedness
Approval	Freedom	Openness
Autonomy	Friendship	Optimism
Balance	Frugality	Patriotism
Beauty	Fulfillment	Peace, nonviolence
Challenge	Fun	Perfection
Change	Generosity	Perseverance
Clarity	Genuineness	Persistence
Cleanliness/orderliness	Goodwill	Personal growth
Collaboration	Goodness	Personal health
Commitment	Gratitude	Pleasure
Communication	Hard work	Power
Community	Harmony	Practicality
Compassion	Healing	Privacy
Competence	Honesty	Problem-solving
Competition	Honor	Professionalism
Concern for others	Improvement	Progress

Confidence	Independence	Prosperity
Connection	Individuality	Punctuality
Conservation	Initiative	Purpose
Content over form	Inner peace	Straightforwardness
Cooperation	Innovation	Strength
Coordination	Integrity	Success
Creativity	Intelligence	Systemization
Credibility	Intensity	Teamwork
Decisiveness	Intimacy	Tolerance
Democracy	Intuition	Tradition
Determination	Joy	Tranquility
Discipline	Justice	Trust
Discovery	Knowledge	Truth
Diversity	Leadership	Unity
Education	Learning	Variety
Efficiency	Love	Vitality
Environment	Loyalty	Wealth
Equality	Meaning	Wisdom
Excellence	Merit	
Exploration	Moderation	

The last step to this exercise is the most important. Pick one of the highlighted and circled values. Start with just one for now. Consider: What is one small step that you can take today to feel like you are living this value? For example: I did this exercise recently with a client who was reflecting on the value of family as being something very important to her and something that she has some control over, in various aspects. We brainstormed together how she can act on this value in a way that brings her pleasure and joy and fills her emotional bank. Earlier in the session, she had been sharing how much she misses her young nephews, who live in a different state. By the end of the session, she had come up with the idea and committed to going home and spending some time crafting some cards to send out in the mail to them. With your sensitivity as one of your biggest strengths, you'll also notice that it adds color to these kinds of activities. If your sensitivity makes you someone who loves more deeply, for example, your nephews in another state are going to feel that in the cards you send, the phone calls you make, and the holidays you spend together.

To take all this a step further, go back to the first exercise in this chapter, and consider: What are you going to prioritize from your pleasurable activities list based on your values? What's most important to you? If your volunteer work and getting a massage both give you the same amount of pleasure, but one is more aligned with your values, the activity aligned with your values is going to give you more emotional bang for your buck. That's because your values and goals are the keys to building your life worth living, a life that helps you feel energized, excited, joyful, and contented; moving through the above exercises is the act of connecting your values and goals.

Your Goals

The above exercises help you accumulate positive experiences and pleasant emotions short term, which is going to accumulate and pay off long term, too. But DBT teaches that playing the long game and thinking big picture about how to bring pleasant experiences into your life, and about your goals, is equally important. Through this next section, I'll help you identify some of your long-term goals and then come up with an action plan to help you start working toward them. This is another important way to fill your emotional bank.

If you know your values, you know where you're headed in life. Having this kind of direction is a kind of emotional insurance; it provides stability and confidence and a sense of pleasure and peace. For example, let's say you home in on tradition as being a value that's very important to you. By focusing on this, you conclude that you want to be more involved with your synagogue during the religious holidays. If you don't take the time to recognize your values, how do you know that you're supposed to be involved with your church, working on your paintings, connecting with your family, running marathons, or whatever the thing is? And once you know that you're supposed to be doing those things and you start doing them, how do you think you'll feel? Probably pretty satisfied, right? What do you think this will do for your overall emotional well-being?

With a fuller emotional bank, your sensitivity will feel more like a genuine strength, as you have more to protect you, more to withdraw from so to speak, as you explore the depths of your emotions and tune in more to them. This creates a cycle, also leaving space for you to learn about your values and plan ways to work toward your goals.

Especially being highly sensitive, there are some unique challenges that may have prevented you from working toward your goals in the past. Perhaps you have many different interests, multiple things that pull you in, making it hard to focus on one goal. Perhaps you're sensitive to perceived rejection or failure and the emotions those bring, making it hard to take the sometimes scary but necessary steps forward to reach your goals. You are definitely not the only one to struggle with this, which is why DBT advises that the first step in working toward your goals is to avoid avoiding.

Avoid Avoiding

What emotions come up for you as you think about taking the first step toward an important personal goal? Let's say the answer is fear. As an HSP, you likely feel that fear acutely. It's intense and maybe pretty uncomfortable. It might be so big, so uncomfortable, that it leaves you feeling frozen in your tracks. This is where some of your other DBT skills can really come in handy. While your emotions have lots of very important and valuable information, they aren't factual, so it's worth "checking the facts," as we say in DBT, and then using opposite action as needed. This is a great opportunity to practice getting comfortable with discomfort and expanding your window of tolerance, especially in the name of something that's deeply important to you.

If the fear could talk, it might say something along the lines of, "This is really important." The fear is just trying to tell you that the stakes feel really high because this is such an important thing to you, personally. But you knew that already. That was the whole point in moving through the values exercise and figuring out what goals are important to you and connected to your personal values. So while the fear is valid, it might not be based in any facts, and you don't necessarily need to act on it. Instead, to move forward with your goals and create your "life worth living," you can give yourself the validation and comfort of knowing that your fear is valuable because it's trying to send you a message, and it's just trying to help you out by drawing attention to just how important these goals really are.

Let's say, for example, that you identify a goal of finding a new job that helps you feel like you're contributing to the well-being of the people in your community and is more aligned with your values. Switching jobs is a scary prospect. Your fear is likely putting thoughts in your head like: *What if I apply to different places and no one wants me? What if I start a new job and I don't know what I'm doing or don't like the people I work with? What if I have to choose between a job aligned with my values and sacrificing my good pay and benefits?* These are totally valid fears, and none of these fear-based thoughts necessarily indicate that it's not a good idea to look for a new job. Fear can also pop up when something feels like a daunting, overwhelming task, and finding a new job can certainly feel like a monstrous task. That's where the goal-planning exercise can come in handy.

Goal-Planning Exercise

The following exercise can help you begin to work toward your goals after you've identified them. Once you've considered your values and what's important to you, start by identifying one goal that you want to work toward. It can be a big project that takes a significant amount of time (like, say, writing a book, going back to school, changing jobs), or it can be something a little more short term or smaller scale (such as reading a book a month, taking a new class, or visiting one new place in your city each week). You'll use the same steps regardless.

For this exercise, we'll use the above example of finding a new job that helps others in your community. As we work through this example, pick a goal of your own and see if you can follow the steps in your journal.

The first step is to write out the required action steps. These are the things you need to do in order to reach your goal. Brainstorm as many as you can, and then add to the list as you run into roadblocks or think of more. For this example, it might look something like this:

- Gain relevant volunteer experience.

- Clean up my resume.

- Practice networking with someone who has a job I admire.

- Pick three places to send job applications to.

- Research companies that have openings and whose work interests me.

Pick the action step that needs to happen first. For example, if you don't think you'll get the job you want without the relevant volunteer experience, start there. Once you've picked the first action step, ask yourself the following questions: Is this step actionable, meaning, do I know what I need to do to get this done? Is it clear what needs to get done? Is this step relevant to what I want to accomplish? And is it realistic for me to accomplish this? You might need to develop more action steps once you home in on where you want to start. For example, gaining volunteer experience might be a big undertaking. You might need to put some thought and planning into how you'll work it into your busy schedule or research where you want to volunteer.

Take small steps toward your goals. Once you have a map of what steps you need to take, break it up into bite-sized pieces so that you can feel accomplished and thus motivated to take the next step, and then the next. Keep repeating these steps until you've met your goal.

Moving Forward

As an emotionally sensitive person who is deeply attuned to the world and those around you, you have a great deal to offer others. You pick up on things that others don't, and you're likely empathetic, passionate, and curious. By tuning in to your values and working toward your goals, you're not only doing a service to yourself, but to those around you, too. Knowing your values and goals is an important piece of taking care of yourself, and the more you can do to take care of yourself, the better able you'll be to offer your strengths and gifts to the world around you. In the next chapter, we'll continue to explore all that you can do to take care of yourself and set yourself up to be as emotionally resilient as possible so that you can continue to use your sensitivity as a strength.

Chapter 9

Taking Care of Yourself First

Body Health for Emotional Health

This next chapter covers something that you do and think about every single day: taking care of your body and your physical health. While this is a task and skill you're already acutely aware of, it's worth visiting important aspects of this because your physical health is so closely tied to your emotional health. You can think of taking care of your body as additional insurance against high emotional reactivity and painful emotions. If you're taking good care of your physical health, it'll be significantly easier to regulate your emotions. The easier it is to regulate your emotions, the easier time you'll have using your sensitivity as a strength and helping your emotions work for you rather than against you.

DBT specifically asks people to focus on these areas of physical health: eating, exercise, sleep, avoiding mood-altering drugs, being sure to stay on top of doctor's appointments to treat any physical illness, being proactive about staying healthy (Linehan 2014). While we'll talk a bit about each of these, as a therapist who specializes in disordered eating, I have many thoughts on the first two areas, especially. There is a strong correlation between disordered eating (as well as substance abuse) and emotional sensitivity. While not everyone who is emotionally sensitive will struggle with addiction or an eating disorder, most who struggle with those issues are highly sensitive. As you think back on the earlier chapters in this book, perhaps you identified issues with food or drugs as one of the ways big emotions come out sideways if they feel too uncomfortable or unmanageable. If this is the case, this chapter may be especially helpful. Regardless of whether this is the case, taking time to tend to your physical self is another way to fill your emotional bank so that you have more to draw on as you practice leaning into, rather than away from, your emotions. In this chapter, we'll explore various strategies that make it easier to tend to your health, and I'll help you identify and remove any barriers that may have been preventing you from doing this before.

I call these skills of tending to physical health "the basics." It's not always particularly groundbreaking stuff, but if you pay attention to what we cover in this chapter, you'll notice a ripple effect as the rest of your life feels a little easier to manage. Taking care of yourself first will decrease those vulnerability factors we talked about in chapter 4 (for example, if you didn't eat enough earlier in the day or if you're running on little sleep, you might feel angrier and more irritable). Additionally, vulnerability factors might be felt more intensely by someone who is highly sensitive.

Elaine Aron points out in her 1995 book that HSPs are more sensitive to stimuli than the average person. This can be external stimuli in your environment (like a loud or busy room), medications, caffeine, exercise, or the internal stimuli of what we feel and experience in our bodies. This means that HSPs are perhaps more affected by hunger, for example. Aron states in her book: "taking good care of a highly sensitive body is like taking care of an infant" (1995, p. 42). When my newborn son wants to eat, or when he's tired, he doesn't hesitate to let us know. As you know if you've been around a newborn, they cry with so much intensity and passion that you'd think their hunger or sleepiness is almost painful. These basic needs require careful attunement and swift attention because babies feel these things acutely. Your needs are similar, because as Aron says, "hunger [for example] is yet another stimulus, from inside," and you feel those stimuli acutely, too. Care for yourself with the same attunement and attention, not despite, but because of your sensitivity, turning toward your feelings and emotions and your needs, rather than away.

Improving Your Relationship with Food and Exercise

How much time do you dedicate to thinking about the food you eat and how you exercise? What's your relationship like with food and your body?

This relationship can easily head south if your natural intuition and inherent ability to take care of your basic needs is corrupted. This can manifest in dieting and eating disorders, for example. Entire books and careers have been dedicated to the subject of diet culture, which, as described by dietitian Christy Harrison, is "a system of beliefs that worships thinness and equates it to health and moral virtue" (2018). Diet culture is oppressive and a "life thief," as Harrison calls it. It dulls other areas of life as people become fixated on having the "right" body. Peeling back layers of trauma related to dieting and body image issues can take years. The good news is that body liberation, thankfully, is becoming a bit more in vogue, and there's a plethora of resources available to you as you work to heal your relationship with food and your body. Go into this process with an open mind, assessing what is and is not working for you in terms of your relationship with food and exercise, and take it easy on yourself as you do the work gradually. Being a highly sensitive person means that you are also highly sensitive to the effects of diet culture and its oppression, and healing can be a long and winding road.

Some good news about exploring diet culture as an HSP is that your passion, sensitivity, and attunement to your values can create a rewarding experience as you work to dismantle the oppression of diet culture. It's an opportunity for your strengths as an HSP to shine as you turn toward your true values, instead of relying on diet culture to guide you. Harrison's description of diet culture as a "life thief" means that it distracts you from your "life worth living" values and goals. With the work outlined in this section, you can not only take better care of your physical body, but also create more space to focus on all you have to offer the world as a highly sensitive person.

Intuitive Eating

I promote intuitive eating with many of my clients, and I'm thankful that it's found significant popularity over the last several years, despite its having been around since the mid-1990s. Intuitive eating was developed by two registered dieticians, and it's an evidence-based framework that integrates "instinct, emotion, and rational thought" to help you reframe attitudes about eating, as well as how you go about getting your basic biological needs met (Tribole 2019). It's founded in dismantling diet culture, and it helps you break away from food rules and give you more flexibility in your relationship with food, thus creating more freedom and joy in your life. If you didn't spend as much time thinking about what you eat and what your body looks like, what other hobbies, interests, and goals would you be making room for? Intuitive eating may be a particularly good fit for you as an HSP because it relies on interoception to tune in to your hunger and fullness cues and intuit what you want to eat. It is also important to note that intuitive eating generally isn't a good fit for people in recovery from an eating disorder, as your hunger and fullness cues may be off. Working with a therapist or dietician who specializes in this area can be helpful.

As we discussed earlier, with practice, interoception can be another strength you possess as an HSP, a skill that comes more easily to you as someone who is sensitive and better attuned to various stimuli. In short, intuitive eating can help significantly in healing a disordered relationship with food, especially as an HSP. Your intuition is strong. The fourth edition of the intuitive eating book, as well as the corresponding workbook, can help you explore these concepts in detail if you'd like more guidance.

Here are some questions to ask yourself that may help you identify a disordered relationship with food:

- Have you devoted a lot of time and energy to trying different diets?

- Do you frequently moralize food (for example, calling certain foods "bad" or "good")?

- Do you have many food rules (such as not eating after a certain time, or only eating certain amounts)?

- Do you have an intense fear of gaining weight?

- Do you ever skip meals or snacks, even if you're hungry?

- Do you ever eat far past the point of fullness, or eat to stave off boredom? Similarly, do you frequently eat to help yourself cope with sadness, fear, or anger?

Self-reflection: Take a few moments to reflect in your journal on one area related to food and eating that you are currently dissatisfied with. For example, let's say you run a pretty busy schedule and frequently put off having a snack or meal. As you reflect on this, perhaps you notice the ways in which this makes you more vulnerable to intense emotions that start to take over. By the time you reach your afternoon without a substantial meal, you're irritable and foggy-headed. What's one thing you can do to start to address this? It may be as simple as packing something the night before or purchasing what I call "see and grab" foods that are easy to take and eat on the go. It might be a bit more complicated; perhaps you need to address underlying fears about adding more food to your diet. Take some time to reflect on this.

Next, consider: If you improved your relationship with food and could put less energy into worrying about what you're eating, what would you have more room for in your life? Which one of your strengths as an HSP would be easier to tap into?

Joyful Movement

Joyful movement is a concept taken from intuitive eating that can help you heal your relationship with exercise. It asks you to expand your definition of exercise beyond the gym or a traditional workout routine to help your relationship with exercise be not only more enjoyable, but also more well-rounded, healthy, and sustainable in the long run.

It's no secret that exercise is important for your physical health and can significantly impact your mood. In fact, studies have shown that regular exercise can be just as effective as taking an antidepressant (Netz 2017). (But seriously, if you need antidepressants, please take them as prescribed.) What happens, though, when your workout routine and time in the gym begins to rule your life, or when you become so fixated on putting hours on the treadmill that exercise feels like a punishment or chore? Ask yourself, do you ever exercise to "make up for" what you eat? This isn't sustainable, or good for your mental health. You deserve to have movement of your body be a joyful, liberating experience that's based on your values and interests, rather than one that's based on fear or diet culture. Especially as an HSP who is creative and naturally drawn to many interests, joyful movement will improve your life.

We're meant to be moving our bodies, and as you heal your relationship with exercise and movement, you might even notice that your body craves movement. One benefit of the concept of joyful movement is that it creates more space for many types of bodies and is inclusive of so many kinds of movement that virtually anyone can practice. Here are just a few examples of what some might consider joyful movement:

- Doing chair yoga

- Having a dance party

- Playing Frisbee

- Taking a snowboarding or skiing lesson

- Hiking

- Taking a walk

- Riding a bike

- Gardening

- Playing Nintendo Wii

- Playing with your dog

- Playing with your children

- Taking a martial arts class

- Horseback riding

- Swimming or jumping in a lake

It doesn't matter how you move your body; the important thing is that you do it. So, find something that feels joyful, energizing, and sustainable for you. Use your passion as an HSP to find something that you love. And if you have struggled to maintain a relationship with exercise because you feel limited in your body, or if the relationship has been damaged by diet culture, there is a wonderful resource called Joyn that is meant to help you start to rebuild that relationship. Joyn is a virtual platform that offers exercise videos and routines for people of all shapes, sizes, and abilities. You can find their videos on their YouTube channel. Also seek help from a therapist or coach whom you trust, or ask your friends to practice joyful movement with you.

> **Self-reflection:** What is your relationship with exercise currently like? Virtually nonexistent? Bordering on obsessive and dominating your calendar? Or somewhere in between? How do you feel when you think about exercise and movement? What changes do you think might make your relationship with exercise more joyful, sustainable, and based on your values, interests, and goals?

Drugs and Alcohol

Being highly sensitive means that you may be more sensitive than the average person to any kind of mood-altering substances, to any kind of stimuli. This includes recreational drugs, alcohol, caffeine, and medication. If your goal is to have an easier time working with your emotions, rather than feeling like your emotions are working against you, or feeling like your sensitivity is a liability, it's worth looking at your relationship with drugs and alcohol. Depending on how you use substances, it could be getting in the way of your ability to make friends with your emotions, as it totally changes how you experience your emotions, and has an impact on your overall health.

It's no secret that drugs and alcohol influence your mood. Alcohol is a depressant, and you might notice your mood dip after you drink, just like you might notice your anxiety spike after drinking caffeine or using certain drugs. This can get in the way of using some of the skills we've outlined thus far in this book. Anxiety and depression can tell us all sorts of lies; it can worm its way in and put all sorts of nonsensical thoughts in our head that sure feel true but are ultimately coming from emotions rather than facts. A depressant or a stimulant can pull you further down this path and then make it harder to get out by using skills such as DBT's model for describing emotions. And the more your physical health is compromised by substances, the worse you'll feel overall, which will also affect your ability to be skillful in difficult situations. It turns into a vicious cycle.

None of this is meant to be sanctimonious nonsense; I do indeed enjoy a drink or two from time to time. I also go through periods where I decide not to drink because I want to have an easier time regulating my mood, I want to be more alert and aware of my surroundings, or it's part of an overall effort to take better care of my physical health. Some people also stay sober because of a painful family history and trauma related to drinking. There are many, many reasons why people might decide to change their relationship with alcohol or drugs, and if you think it may benefit you, it's worth considering changes that will make it easier to work toward your goals. This is also a pretty tall order, and if needed, there are specialists that can help. If you've become reliant on it, alcohol specifically can be deadly to withdraw from and requires specialized care. Minor problems with drugs and alcohol will require minor solutions and adjustments, so if you're having more than minor problems, do not place the expectation and pressure on yourself to successfully make changes just by using the self-reflection below.

Big, difficult emotions may have left you feeling like you needed fast-acting solutions (such as various substances) to help you manage, which is very valid. If your sensitivity felt overwhelming and hard to deal with, of course you're going to use whatever resources you have easily and readily available to you. But just because your sensitivity may have created challenges doesn't mean your sensitivity was ever a bad thing. There is always opportunity to start practicing different, more effective skills to manage big emotions so that you can begin to see the gifts that they can bring.

> **Self-reflection:** If you are someone who uses any kind of substances, which substance is having the biggest impact on your mood or overall health? How can you tell that it's impacting you? Do you have any goals for changing your relationship with this substance, and if so, what is one small change that you can make this week to start you on the path of meeting this goal?

Sleep

We do it each day, and it's a vital part of our mental and physical health. Sleep is how we repair our muscles and the cells in our body, boost our immune system, and help our brains process memories and emotions. You've certainly had the experience of being much more susceptible to intense emotions because you're running on little sleep. Sleep is often neglected by many people, and all of us have times when we skimp on sleep. Regularly getting good sleep is not something you will do perfectly. Far from it. But insofar as you can make gradual, small improvements to your sleep over time, the better equipped you will be to work with your emotions and use your sensitivity as a strength as you go into situations sharper and ready to use your skills.

Sleep hygiene is a set of behavioral and environmental changes that can help you improve your sleep. It includes:

- Keeping your room totally dark as you go to sleep

- Not using any electronics 30-60 minutes before bed

- Having a soothing routine before bed

- Keeping a cool temperature in your room

- Getting some movement and sunlight during the day

- Avoiding caffeine and naps too late in the day

Consider: Is there one thing from this list that you haven't tried that you can start to practice even just one night a week? How might such a change improve your mood and your overall well-being? If you regularly practice habits like these and still struggle with sleep, talk to your doctor and possibly consider a sleep study in which a professional can assess your sleep in detail.

Your Health Is Not Your Worth

Each one of us will, at some point in our lives, experience health issues that we have no control over. This is just part of living in a fallible, human body. It may feel like a failing, even if it is not, and struggling with your health will impact the other areas of your life and make it hard to work with your emotions. This will be a huge challenge on its own on top of the already hard work of taking care of yourself. Remember to maintain balance in your life by not falling into a pit of orthorexia (an obsession with healthy eating), pushing yourself beyond your limits with exercise, or generally chasing perfectionism as you work to take care of your body. Chasing perfectionism will dull or take away energy from other areas of your life. Avoiding this work altogether will also zap your energy and dull your light. Help this process be something that adds to your life rather than takes away. Be gentle and gracious with yourself. Understand that any habits you've developed thus far are habits you developed for a reason as you worked to get by. Especially as an HSP, it can be easy to rely on quick fixes like substances or disordered eating to help you cope. Using other skills instead may sometimes feel harder in the short term, but will ultimately be easier in the long term, as you'll feel better mentally and physically.

Self-Reflection: Reflect on what areas of physical health you feel you have a handle on, and what you need to focus on more. What's preventing you from focusing on those areas? Where do you perhaps need more balance? What's getting in the way of finding that balance?

Moving Forward

As you make changes slowly, gradually, and graciously with yourself, know that for most people, it is hard to build new habits, and as an HSP you may be sensitive to change. Gradual work is how you will make changes that you're able to sustain long term, changes that will benefit you for years to come.

Your sensitivity and the strengths that come with it lend themselves to doing the work in this chapter. You're likely more creative, and you can use your creativity to your benefit as you work on adjusting how you care for your body. Chase creativity rather than perfectionism as you figure out how to enjoy food, what joyful movement means for you as you explore your passions and interests, and how you can help your body feel energized and cared for. Being sensitive also gives you an attunement to your emotions that can make you more skilled at practicing what you've learned in this book. Remember that one of the biggest gifts your emotions can bring are messages and important information about what you need. Tune in to what your emotions are trying to tell you, and then use that information to give your mind and your body whatever it is you're needing in that moment. Being attuned to your physical and emotional needs is another way to practice using your sensitivity as a strength.

Conclusion

Emotion Regulation Long Term for a Happier You

One of my main goals in writing this book is to help you feel empowered as an emotionally sensitive person. Your sensitivity is a wealth of gifts and strengths, waiting to be tapped into. Your creativity, focus, passion, intuition, and depth of feeling and perception have so much to offer the world and those around you. These strengths will help you accomplish great things. Your sensitivity and deep emotions also have wisdom. Sometimes we just need a little extra support and guidance to hear that wisdom. My hope is that the DBT skills in this book provide that support.

If you can make friends with your emotions and see big emotions as a strength, you will begin to see all the gifts that emotions themselves have to give. Even the most painful emotions, like sadness, anger, or guilt, have gifts, as they can teach you about what's very important to you, and they can even help motivate you. Your emotions can tell you what you're needing and where to head next. If you turn away from those emotions, or try to stuff them down, they'll just try to find a new way to be heard. They're on your team, trying to work with you, to your benefit. The more you can see your emotions as a gift and turn toward them, the more easily you can make friends with your emotions and work with them, rather than feeling like they're working against you. Once you can start to do this, you will see the rewards. As you understand better what your emotions are trying to tell you, painful emotions become a little less intense or don't last quite as long, and you can feel some relief. You can tolerate more. Your relationships become a little easier, and you become better at using words to describe your experiences, or simply tuning in to your body when words are not enough. The skills you've learned in this book will get a little easier. As it gets easier, your confidence will grow, and it'll be clearer that your emotional sensitivity is a gift, a great superpower.

My other hope for you is that as you use the skills in this book, and perhaps make some changes to how you tend to your emotions and interact with the world around you, you do so with self-compassion and kindness. It is hard to be emotionally sensitive. At times, it's a trait that is underappreciated, or even belittled. Perhaps when you picked up this book, you were a bit skeptical, but also curious about how to use your sensitivity to your benefit. That place of curiosity is a great place to be, as it'll keep you learning. Learning about yourself and your emotions is an ongoing process without a definitive end. Naturally, there will be bumps in the road as you run into new challenges. To make this work sustainable and continue practicing these skills long term, you'll have to have some compassion and grace with yourself. Remember your self-validation skills, and to chase progress rather than perfection so as not to make things harder on yourself.

Your sensitivity is a gift to others, and it is your superpower, so go forward with confidence.

Acknowledgments

Thank you to Georgia Kolias, whose patience, guidance, and support over the past few years have helped me grow as a writer. To Vicraj Gill, who helped whip this book into shape and provided invaluable feedback. To the rest of the New Harbinger team for all they've done to bring this book into the world. To Jaime Castillo, who has mentored me through so many professional milestones. To the rest of the Find Your Shine team: I couldn't ask for better colleagues or friends. To my clients, for trusting me with so much, giving me my dream job, and teaching me so much more than I could ever teach them. To my dad, who gave me my start as an author at Lauer Publishing in Brooklyn many years ago. To my mom, who has built me up my whole life and helped me believe that I'm capable of having anything I chase after. To Erich: I love you dearly and you bring me so much joy. To the rest of my family, for their unending support and love. My mom and my mother-in-law both helped tremendously with our newborn while I worked on getting more than two consecutive hours of sleep and finishing the final manuscript of this book. To Travis: We have shared so much love and so many adventures over the years, and my gratitude for all you've done to support me and our little family is endless. And lastly, to Elliott: You are a dream come true. Thank you for being the one to make me a mom.

Resources

If you're struggling, don't hesitate to reach out to a professional therapist. Many mental health struggles such as obsessive-compulsive disorder (OCD), eating disorders, post-traumatic stress disorder (PTSD), and substance abuse require specific, specialized treatment from trained professionals. Thankfully, there are many resources available to help you find a professional for any mental health struggles you may be dealing with.

For help finding an eating disorder therapist, you can visit nationaleatingdisorders.org.

The Substance Abuse and Mental Health Services Administration (SAMHSA)'s national hotline is: 1-800-662-4357.

To find a therapist who specializes in DBT, head to either https://behavioraltech.org/resources/find-a-therapist-app or https://dbt-lbc.org/index.hp?page=101163.

Psychology Today can be used to search for providers based on zip code, specialty, cost, and whether they take your insurance. Open Path Collective is another directory that can specifically help with finding reduced-cost therapy. Often, if you call the number on the back of your health insurance card, you can let them know that you're looking for a list of covered providers in your area, and they will email you a list. If you reach out to a therapist and they are not accepting new clients, they can often refer you to a trusted colleague who is. As of July 2022, you can reach the National Suicide Prevention Lifeline by simply dialing 988. You can also go to suicidepreventionlifeline.org for more.

References

Aron, E. 1995. *The Highly Sensitive Person: How to Thrive When the World Overwhelms You*. New York: Three Rivers Press.

Feldman Barrett, L. "Try These Two Smart Techniques to Help You Master Your Emotions." *Ted*, June 21, 2018. https://ideas.ted.com/try-these-two-smart-techniques-to-help-you-master-your-emotions.

Harrison, C. "What Is Diet Culture?" *Christy Harrison* (blog), March 8, 2019. https://christyharrison.com/blog/what-is-diet-culture.

Kashdan, T. B., L. Feldman Barrett, and P. E. McKnight. 2015. "Unpacking Emotion Differentiation: Transforming Unpleasant Experience by Perceiving Distinctions in Negativity." *Current Directions in Psychological Science* 24(1): 10–16. https://doi.org/10.1177/0963721414550708.

Linehan, M. M. 1993. *Cognitive-Behavioral Treatment of Borderline Personality Disorder*. New York: Guilford Publications.

———. 2014. *DBT Skills Training Handouts and Worksheets*, 2nd ed. New York: Guilford Publications.

McKay, M., J. C. Wood, and J. Brantlee. 2019. *The Dialectical Behavior Therapy Skills Workbook*, 2nd ed. Oakland, CA: New Harbinger Publications.

Netz, Y. 2017. "Is the Comparison Between Exercise and Pharmacologic Treatment of Depression in the Clinical Practice Guideline of the American College of Physicians Evidence-Based?" *Frontiers in Pharmacology* 8: 257. https://doi.org/10.3389/fphar.2017.00257.

Siegel, D. J. 2012. *The Developing Mind: How Relationships and the Brain Interact to Shape Who We Are*, 2nd ed. New York: Guilford Press.

Tribole, E. "Definition of Intuitive Eating." *Intuitive Eating.* July 17, 2019. https://www.intuitiveeating.org/definition-of-intuitive-eating.

University of British Columbia. "How Your Brain Reacts to Emotional Information Is Influenced by Your Genes." *ScienceDaily.* Accessed December 6, 2021. http://www.sciencedaily.com/releases/2015/05/150507135919.htm.

Emma Lauer, LCSW, is a therapist specializing in the treatment of eating disorders, self-harming behaviors, and trauma. Emma is an eye movement desensitization and reprocessing (EMDR)-certified therapist, and has taught at Arizona State University. She currently practices therapy and oversees interns and other staff therapists as clinical supervisor at Find Your Shine Therapy, a group private practice in Tempe, AZ.

Real change *is* possible

For more than forty-five years, New Harbinger has published proven-effective self-help books and pioneering workbooks to help readers of all ages and backgrounds improve mental health and well-being, and achieve lasting personal growth. In addition, our spirituality books offer profound guidance for deepening awareness and cultivating healing, self-discovery, and fulfillment.

Founded by psychologist Matthew McKay and Patrick Fanning, New Harbinger is proud to be an independent, employee-owned company. Our books reflect our core values of integrity, innovation, commitment, sustainability, compassion, and trust. Written by leaders in the field and recommended by therapists worldwide, New Harbinger books are practical, accessible, and provide real tools for real change.

newharbingerpublications

MORE BOOKS from
NEW HARBINGER PUBLICATIONS